David Morris

Agile Project Management

3rd Edition

In easy steps is an imprint of In Easy Steps Limited
16 Hamilton Terrace · Holly Walk · Leamington Spa
Warwickshire · United Kingdom · CV32 4LY
www.ineasysteps.com

Third Edition

Notice of Liability
Every effort has been made to ensure that this book contains accurate
and current information. However, In Easy Steps Limited and the
authors shall not be liable for any loss or damage suffered by readers
as a result of any information contained herein.

Trademarks
All trademarks are acknowledged as belonging to their respective
companies.

In Easy Steps Limited supports The Forest Stewardship Council (FSC),
the leading international forest certification organisation. All our titles
that are printed on Greenpeace approved FSC certified paper carry the
FSC logo.

MIX
Paper from
responsible sources
FSC® C020837

Printed and bound in the United Kingdom

ISBN 978-1-84078-974-4

Contents

9   Agile projects with lean principles   129

10   Agile in controlled environments   143

11   From projects to continual flow   157

1 Introducing agile projects

This chapter provides the background to the need for an agile approach to projects. It covers the benefits of using an agile approach and an overview of four frameworks for leading agile projects.

For a basic introduction to project management, refer to our book **Effective Project Management in easy steps**.

Templates are available on our website for many common project documents. Please visit **https://ineasysteps.com/downloads/**

All pages that include an example from **Vanguard Power** – the energy company used for illustration – are highlighted with this transmission tower/pylon in the margin.

Introduction

This book was written for everyone curious about how project management is affected by agile principles and practices. The primary audience is likely to be experienced project managers looking to broaden their knowledge and skills to lead agile projects. It will also be of interest to developers and others already working on agile projects who wish to understand the role of project management.

Learning agile project management in stages

As with any capability, your ability to lead agile projects will develop over time as you gain more experience and knowledge.

- **Novice**: On your first agile projects, it will feel safer to find and follow a set path of best-practice guidelines – this book can be an essential companion for you on that journey.

- **Proficient**: As your knowledge and experience grows, you will start to recognize patterns and understand how to mix and combine techniques – this book compares four project management frameworks, with guidance on when to use each.

- **Expert**: Once you have experienced leading agile projects in a wide range of conditions, you will start to contribute to practice improvement – Chapter 14 focuses on the evolution of project management.

Learning agile project management in easy steps

The **In Easy Steps** series of books is designed to take readers step-by-step through a new topic – learning through the experience of doing, rather than forcing you to work your way through pages of theory and being left to find your own way.

The best way to experience agile project management is to work on an agile project and learn first-hand by doing it. For those who want to find out about agile project management beforehand, the next best way is to see it play out step-by-step. This book guides you through a whole project life-cycle, from initiation through discovery, delivery, and learning, to closure.

To illustrate this, as you work your way through the book you will also be following the experience of a fictitious energy business – called **Vanguard Power** – that have realized they need to develop more consumer-facing services alongside maintaining and growing their infrastructure.

About agile project management

This first chapter provides an introduction to agile projects, beginning with some of the challenges we face in today's business environment, and how an agile approach helps cope with them.

Leading agile projects
Preparing to lead agile projects asks more of us than just learning some new practices; it **fundamentally changes our role**. Chapter 2 explores the impact on project management responsibilities.

The life-cycle of an agile project
These changes are brought to life stepping through a full project.

Chapter 3 describes how to **set good foundations**, forming a team, agreeing outcomes, gaining funds, and getting started.

Chapters 4 to 6 follow the repeating cycles of **discovery**, **delivery**, and **learning** that characterize an agile project.

Finally, Chapter 7 covers how we **close out** an agile project.

Frameworks for agile project management
The next five chapters present a range of agile project frameworks.

Chapter 8 defines the **Agile Project Framework** – a standard based on the Dynamic Systems Development Method.

Chapter 9 describes how to apply **lean principles and practices** to leading agile projects.

Chapter 10 explores how to overcome the challenges of leading agile projects in more **controlled environments**.

Chapter 11 considers the differences in organizations that have moved **from projects to continual flow** of delivery.

Chapter 12 describes approaches for **leading agile projects at scale**.

Frameworks for agile delivery
Agile project frameworks should also be capable of working with complementary delivery approaches. Chapter 13 covers five **agile delivery approaches,** with guidance on how they might be implemented or even combined.

Trends in agile project management
As the project management profession continues to evolve, Chapter 14 explores the impact of **current and future trends**.

The need for a shift in mindset

The profession of project management evolved from traditional construction and manufacturing industries, where requirements were commonly locked down early, solutions were well defined, and customers were accustomed to seeing nothing until the end.

While this was accepted practice for many years, such a predictive approach does not suit the challenges our organizations face today. We need a more adaptive approach to help cope with the disruption caused by the pace of change in technology, consumer expectations, population growth, and climate change.

To determine when we need a more adaptive approach, we need a way to make sense of our organizational context and our project deliverables. The following two models have been proven to reliably help assess and guide our choice of approach.

Assessing our organization's context

The **Cynefin Framework** was developed to help make sense of our situation and guide which approach might suit making changes.

The *Cynefin Framework* was developed by Dave Snowden. *Cynefin* is a Welsh word meaning habitat or domain.

- In **clear** situations, once we can see the problem, the solution is simple and obvious – suiting a *checklist* approach.

- In **complicated** situations, there may be more than one solution; we typically have to uncover the way forward through detailed analysis or consulting an expert – suiting a more *predictive plan-driven* approach.

- In more **complex** situations, we cannot observe or analyze a way forward; instead, we need to feel our way a step at a time – suiting a more *adaptive exploratory feedback-driven* approach.

- Finally, in **chaotic** situations, such as a pandemic or global financial crises, we first need to stabilize our organization before we can make any changes – suiting a *rapid response* or *immediate action*.

Assessing our project's deliverables

The **Pace-Layered Application Strategy** was developed to help inform an approach to managing projects, by categorizing the deliverables of a project.

The *Pace-Layered Application Strategy* helps select an appropriate development approach, based on the type of application.

Pace-Layered Application Strategy

New ideas to gain competitive advantage	Systems of Innovation	High rate of change with Lean Governance
Enhancements to maintain advantage	Systems of Differentiation	Balance of change and governance
Minor change for efficiency & compliance	Systems of Record	High governance with low rate of change

---

- Systems of **Innovation** involve responses to new markets or opportunities, which would suit an exploratory approach that generates feedback and results quickly.

- Systems of **Differentiation** involve unique selling points for existing markets or products, which would suit careful analysis and design combined with fast implementation.

- Systems of **Record** involve mission-critical administration and important transactions, which would suit more standardized processes and compliance with governance.

Choosing the right approach

Assessing our deliverables and context will guide us toward an appropriate approach. When our answer involves innovation and complexity, the *exploratory* and *feedback-driven* requirements mean we need to adopt an agile project management approach.

However, even when the deliverables and context might suit a more *plan-driven* approach, we still benefit from adopting many of the practices outlined in this book, especially in organizations with a portfolio project management approach (see page 174 for portfolios at scale and page 206 for multi-speed delivery).

While the energy sector is mature, **Vanguard Power** do not currently have any consumer-facing services. As developing this would involve some risk, they chose to adopt agile project management so that they could deliver some services earlier and get feedback that would help them improve.

The name of the *Scrum* framework can be traced back to Takeuchi and Nonaka coining the term *rugby approach*.

A more adaptive approach

The shift from plan-driven to adaptive feedback-driven approaches to project management also involves a mindset shift.

> "The traditional sequential *relay race* approach to product development – exemplified by phased program planning – may conflict with the goals of maximum speed and flexibility. Instead, a holistic or rugby approach – where a team tries to go the distance as a unit, passing the ball back and forth – may better serve today's competitive requirements."
> *Takeuchi and Nonaka, Harvard Business Review, 1986*

Plan-driven project management
A plan-driven approach to project management typically starts with a detailed specification of scope and deliverables, after which, time and cost can be estimated. Once formed, the team will analyze, design, and build the deliverables, which they test to confirm as meeting the requirements. Finally, they present all finished deliverables, which may or may not be accepted as matching the specification. Such a predictive approach suits less novel systems in more stable situations where the requirements are unlikely to change and the technical solution is well known.

Feedback-driven project management
A feedback-driven approach, on the other hand, accepts that requirements may not be known in advance and will continue to emerge. Instead of fixing the scope, we fix the size of the team and the amount of time (and thus cost) we are willing to invest, and then reprioritize requirements as we discover them. Such an adaptive approach suits the higher levels of risk when requirements and technology are likely to change, and especially when we need to deliver some part of the scope early. The difference between the two approaches is illustrated below:

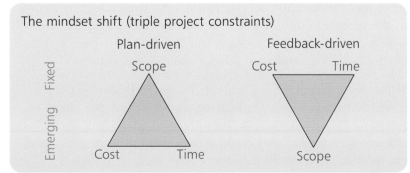

The mindset shift (triple project constraints)

To be effective, this shift also requires some new practices that enable teams to develop with speed, flexibility, and feedback.

The self-organizing autonomous team

Teams should be free to determine the best technology, architecture, and approach to development. Ideally, they should think of themselves like a start-up, taking initiative and defining their own identity. To facilitate this level of autonomy, there should also be clear guidelines, expectations, and checkpoints to provide confidence while avoiding instability, tension, and chaos.

The learning team

As teams grow and discover how to solve their problems, they will experience a range of learning across levels (e.g. individuals, the team, and the wider organization) and across functions (e.g. analysis, programming, and quality assurance). It is vital that this learning is encouraged and that opportunities are also found to transfer this to people outside the team.

Overlapping development stages

The team should work together across all activities, testing one deliverable while building a second deliverable at the same time as planning a third. This is in contrast to the more sequential plan-driven approaches that make a team wait for all requirements to be specified before starting to build anything, for all build work to be completed before starting to test, and for all testing to be completed before anything can be reviewed, as illustrated below:

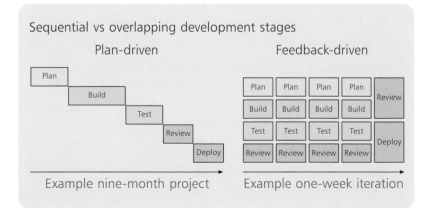

The overlapping stages enable a team to replan or do further build work immediately, when required, rather than waiting.

Agile values and principles

As more adaptive feedback-driven approaches emerged, a group of 14 project management and software development professionals recognized the need for a clear statement that described these alternatives to more predictive plan-driven approaches.

In early 2001, they published this as a manifesto for what they described as **agile software development**.

The *Manifesto for Agile Software Development* was developed in February 2001 at the Snowbird ski resort in Utah, USA.

> **The Agile Manifesto**
>
> We are uncovering better ways of developing software by doing it and helping others do it; through this work we have come to value:
>
> - **Individuals and interactions** over **processes and tools.**
> - **Working solutions** over **comprehensive documentation.**
> - **Customer collaboration** over **contract negotiation.**
> - **Responding to change** over **following a plan.**
>
> That is, while there is value in the items on the right, we value the items on the left more.

The agile values

These four value pairs have come to be known as the **agile values**. The meaning of these is described below:

- **Individuals and interactions**: Treating each other well and facilitating good interactions is more important than following strict protocols or arguing over which tools to use.

- **Working solutions**: Delivering a part of the solution that works is much more useful than investing in requirements documents that will be thrown away – however, documents required for operation and support are still valued.

- **Customer collaboration**: Requirements cannot be fully defined at the beginning of the project, therefore continuous customer involvement is very important.

- **Responding to change**: Agile project management enables a quicker response to new information – like feedback or scope changes – that can create competitive advantage.

12 principles

These values are in turn supported by the following 12 principles:

1   **Customer satisfaction**: by the early and the continuing delivery of useful solutions.

2   **Changing requirements**: welcome changing requirements, even late in the development process.

3   **Frequent delivery**: of working solutions, from every couple of weeks to every couple of months.

4   **Measure of progress**: delivery of working solutions is the principle measurement of progress.

5   **Sustainable development**: so that the sponsors, developers, and users can maintain a steady pace indefinitely.

6   **Close cooperation**: business people and developers must work together daily throughout the project.

7   **Motivated team**: by giving them the support they need and trusting them to get the job done.

8   **Face-to-face conversation**: whether in-person or digital, the most efficient and effective method of conveying information.

9   **Technical excellence**: through continuous attention to quality working and good design.

10   **Simplicity**: by keeping things simple, the amount of work that has to be done is minimized.

11   **Self-organizing teams**: the best architectures, requirements and designs emerge from self-organizing teams.

12   **Regular adaptation**: the team regularly reflect on how to become more effective and adjust their behavior accordingly.

The term *"software"* from the original manifesto is now commonly replaced by *"solution"* to signify these values and principles apply to projects and other work with non-software deliverables.

With the growing popularity (and need) for remote and hybrid teams, digital tools can support communication and collaboration (see pages 198-199).

Don't forget

These benefits are modeled on the Project Management Institute's *project performance domains.*

16

Benefits for project outcomes

Applying these principles to how we plan and lead projects will improve the outcomes of our projects across a number of areas.

Adapting to changing requirements and uncertainty

All projects experience some degree of uncertainty, and any uncertainty presents a risk to project outcomes. Projects dealing with innovation and complexity will face higher levels of risk due to the number of unknowns and likely degree of change.

Agile approaches involve shorter delivery timescales and more frequent planning, so teams are better able to handle unknowns and changes. This is especially useful when customers cannot define their requirements before they have seen a prototype.

Delivering value and results early

Following agile practices will ensure that the project delivers a quality product sooner than on traditional projects. While an early release of a product will not have all required features, teams work to deliver a minimum viable product (MVP) each time, following the Pareto principle of prioritizing the most important features first.

Delivering significant benefits early will contribute to improved outcomes overall. Should the customer decide they have received sufficient functionality and benefit, this also provides them with the option to end the project earlier than planned and free the team up for other high-priority change and improvement work.

Stakeholder and customer involvement

Effective engagement for stakeholders and external customers will improve project outcomes, enabling them to share in making decisions, setting priorities, and resolving problems. Their ongoing involvement will increase their confidence that the final product will meet their requirements, whereas failing to involve them will increase the likelihood of dissatisfaction with the final product.

Transparency and monitoring progress

Using the delivery of working solutions as the principal measure of progress is a principle that anyone involved in a project is likely to appreciate. This makes it easier for the project manager to ensure that deliverables are monitored and reported transparently. The team will continually break their work down into small increments and deliver these frequently. Stakeholders and customers will also be able to see the impact of each release.

Team motivation and wellbeing

By empowering the team to self-organize, they will be motivated to focus more on quality and improved outcomes.

The principles of frequent delivery and time to reflect ensure not only that the pace of work is sustainable but also that the team can learn and improve. While working outside normal business hours still remains a possibility, it should cease to be the default.

Planning to keep options open

Although it may appear that far less effort is invested in planning, it shifts instead from being detailed at initiation to being more continual. Delaying detailed commitments increases flexibility.

Rather than a detailed plan of weekly deliverables, outcomes are typically depicted on a roadmap by quarter, which is reviewed and adapted frequently. A distinct sub-set of deliverables is typically planned once per fortnight, followed by a daily review as progress reveals hidden complexity, new risk, and unexpected blockers.

Adaptive life-cycle

Applying these agile principles to project management requires us to pause frequently, reflect on performance, and consider whether there are any challenges or opportunities to improve our ways of working. This helps foster a learning environment.

Combined with enabling teams to self-organize, this leads to continual improvement in how we deliver working solutions, as well as our communication, engagement, management of physical resources, procurement, and everything else required to keep the project operating smoothly and achieving its outcomes.

Audit and compliance

There is a myth that agile teams do whatever they like, with no documentation or process. If true, this would be a major concern for audit and compliance. However, while the attitude to process and documentation might be lighter, there is still plenty of rigor.

This lighter approach enables a shift:

- From auditing teams against compliance with a rule-book.

- To facilitating and improving how they assess and mitigate risks and impediments.

Agile project frameworks

As there are many approaches, methodologies, and practices that adhere to agile values and principles, these have been simplified into **four frameworks** for this book, summarized below:

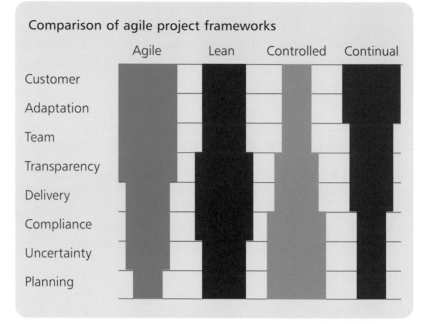

Comparison of agile project frameworks

	Agile	Lean	Controlled	Continual
Customer				
Adaptation				
Team				
Transparency				
Delivery				
Compliance				
Uncertainty				
Planning				

This table compares the four frameworks by depicting the emphasis each gives to the eight project performance domains. These domains were introduced in the previous section on benefits (see pages 16-17) and will be further explored in Chapter 2, while the frameworks are described below and detailed in Chapters 8 to 11.

Agile project management

When projects need an iterative and incremental approach to delivering outcomes, they need an approach with enough planning and oversight to enable delivery of quality products on time and within budget, and that works well with agile delivery frameworks.

The Agile Project Framework (see Chapter 8) is a feedback-driven approach to projects that succeeds by focusing more on customer value, adaptation, team wellbeing, and transparency. While this makes it suited to organizations operating in highly competitive markets or working with novel technologies, it would not be so well suited to developing systems of record or organizations operating in heavily regulated markets.

Lean project management

The lean process approach originated in large-scale manufacturing, where the focus was on minimizing waste and improving flow. It can best be summarized as seven major principles, which are derived from lean manufacturing: eliminate waste (including unnecessary code and functionality); amplify learning; commit as late as possible; deliver as fast as possible; empower the team; build in integrity (so that components work well together); and see the whole (software systems are the product of their interactions).

Agile projects with lean principles (see Chapter 9) is a flow-based approach that succeeds by focusing on smooth flow, quality, and good controls. This makes it suited to projects focused on process improvement, or for organizations in manufacturing or who develop system components.

Agile projects in controlled environments

Large organizations, especially those in government, healthcare, and other regulated industries, are typically unable to remove or reduce much governance and compliance – especially when they are overseen by third parties, such as industry regulators.

Agile projects in controlled environments (see Chapter 10) is a stage-based approach that succeeds by focusing on planning, compliance, and process. This makes it suited to organizations where projects still need to be plan-driven; however, this would likely be too heavy-handed for those in more competitive markets.

Continual product delivery

Some organizations have chosen to prioritize their funding to create a continual flow of value. For them, the stages of project initiation and closure become an unnecessary overhead.

As an alternative to projects, as temporary organization structures to deliver value, they create aligned groups of development teams, approve streams of funding in advance, set clear objectives and goals, and create roles responsible for prioritizing the work that should generate customer value and meet those goals.

From projects to continual flow (see Chapter 11) discusses this product-based approach that succeeds by focusing on value streams, product fit, and continual improvement. This makes it suited to mature service organizations in competitive markets.

Don't forget

This shift toward continual flow over projects started as an online discussion, from which it is also known as *#NoProjects* (the hashtag label on posts and replies on Twitter).

Summary

- This book provides an introduction to leading agile projects, through several different project frameworks, and how to select which is right for your project.

- Traditional projects start by documenting all requirements. Agile projects start by choosing a team size and timeframe, then allow the requirements to emerge during the project.

- Traditional methodology was based on predictive plan-driven approaches, not well suited to complex innovation projects.

- In addition to fixing the requirements too early, traditional methodology also suffered from a lack of customer involvement and an authoritarian style of managing the team.

- As a result of these problems, software developers started to define more lightweight methods.

- These methods were codified in the **Agile Manifesto**, which called for a focus on individuals and interactions, working software, customer collaboration, and responding to change.

- Trying to lead an agile delivery using traditional project management approaches does not work – which is why agile project management frameworks were developed.

- A definition of agile project management was first published by the DSDM Consortium, and this focused on managing a project following the principles of the Agile Manifesto.

- The ideal agile project includes any area where the requirements or technology cannot be known fully in advance.

- Conversely, projects with fixed requirements and solutions may be better managed using traditional methodology.

- A number of frameworks have emerged that mean larger projects and programs can also follow more agile methods.

- There is a growing practice of shifting product development onto an operational footing, rather than within a project.

- Depending on context and deliverables, an agile project is likely to include a combination of practices that support agile projects, lean processes, and working in controlled environments.

2 Leading agile projects

This chapter explores what is involved in leading agile projects, reviewing how agile values and principles are implemented through the eight domains of project performance.

Avoiding project chaos

As we saw in the introduction, the traditional approach to project management of software development projects was largely based on principles from the construction industry, resulting in an inflexible sequential process. The rigid nature of this approach caused many high-profile government and commercial projects to fail or be seriously over budget and time. This was further amplified when the same approach was tried on novel technologies in complex environments.

The chaos of failed projects

The Standish Group have been researching project success factors for over 25 years, assessing more than 50,000 projects on how well they delivered to budget, on time, and with satisfactory outcomes.

● **Successful projects** are completed to agreed timescales, keep within budget, and deliver satisfactory outcomes.

● **Challenged projects** might be late, over budget, with unsatisfactory outcomes, or a combination of all three.

● **Failed projects** are either canceled before delivery or are delivered but never used (a shocking yet common outcome).

Project outcomes by method		
	Feedback-driven (agile)	Plan-driven (waterfall)
Successful	42%	13%
Challenged	47%	59%
Failed	11%	28%

CHAOS Report (Standish Group, 2020)

The final CHAOS Report (2020) showed that agile projects were over three times more likely to succeed and nearly three times less likely to fail. The likelihood of success was even higher in certain sectors, most notably in finance with a ten-fold increase in success.

They also describe the evolution of project management through 20-year stages: "Wild-West" (1960-80), "Waterfall" (1980-2000), "Agile" (2000-), and the advent of "Continual Flow" (see Chapter 11).

Don't forget

The third success factor was originally delivering to scope, but due to the likelihood of continual scope change, a better determinant of success is satisfaction with project outcomes.

Common factors of project success

Based on their 25 years of research, the Standish Group demonstrated how the following factors contribute reliably to project success:

- **Clarity** and **prioritization**: It is critical that those leading discovery have clear business goals and an objective way of prioritizing between competing demands and limited budget.

- **Active involvement at all levels**: From executive sponsorship to end users and customers, it is vital that key roles are engaged, informed, and involved throughout.

- **Healthy team environments** and **good tools**: Striking the right balance between these factors is prominent on successful projects. Teams need access to the right tools and practices, and typically these are standardized across teams, freeing the team to self-organize.

- **Capacity** and **skill levels**: Projects are more successful when the team have the capacity and the skills to do the work required; with greater impact from keeping the pace of work sustainable, then training team members when required.

- **Size of delivery**: On large projects there is a heavy reliance on the expertise of the whole team for success, whereas limiting the size of commitment and delivering more frequently will lead to more success, irrespective of any other factor.

- **Adaptive process**: Projects had more satisfactory outcomes when they focused on transparency, inspection, and adaptation. That is, the current status of everything was easy to see, teams made time to reflect on their effectiveness, and invested in small safe-to-fail trials to test out improvements.

Trump cards for project success

While all these factors will be present to some degree on any type of project, the CHAOS Report considers the two factors with the most impact to be the **size of delivery** and the **ability to adapt**.

Agile project management succeeds by making smaller commitments, keeping options open, and delivering more frequently. When a **minimum viable product** (**MVP**) requires more time to be ready for market, earlier deliveries help elicit constructive feedback from stakeholders to improve usability and quality.

Changing accountabilities

The goal of an agile project is still to deliver on time, to budget, and with satisfactory outcomes. What changes is the emphasis between these three factors, how it gets done, and who is accountable.

Traditionally, project managers were deemed accountable for managing **all aspects** of a project, whereas today many of these have been taken on by other roles (summarized below). This shifts the focus from **managing** a project to **leading** and facilitating the team toward successful outcomes.

These accountabilities are mapped to the Project Management Institute's *project performance domains.*

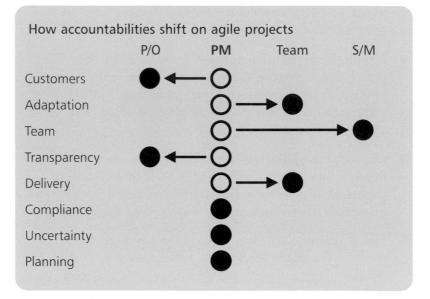

How accountabilities shift on agile projects

	P/O	PM	Team	S/M
Customers	●	○ ←		
Adaptation		○ →	●	
Team		○		→ ●
Transparency	●	○ ←		
Delivery		○ →	●	
Compliance		●		
Uncertainty		●		
Planning		●		

Changing project roles
Agile delivery frameworks have changed or introduced some roles:

- **Product owner** (P/O above): Accountable for representing the voice of the customer and keeping stakeholders informed.

- **Scrum master** (S/M above): Accountable for facilitating team performance and wellbeing.

- **Team**: Although all projects have teams, on agile projects the delivery team are accountable for delivery and adaptation.

Agile teams are also deemed to be collectively responsible for all aspects of project performance. For example, while a team member should be **individually accountable** for the quality of their own work, the team are **jointly responsible** for overall quality. This is designed to foster collaboration and collective problem-solving.

Agile teams are to be encouraged to resolve their own challenges (with support).

Stakeholder and customer engagement

On any project, engaging well with stakeholders and customers is key to successful outcomes. On agile projects, the accountability for this now sits with the *product owner* role (or its equivalent).

Adaptation of product and process

For novel technologies in complex environments, the *team* have to seek feedback and adapt the product, and pause frequently to reflect on performance and adapt their approach where necessary.

Fostering environments for a healthy team

Agile teams need an environment that enables self-organization, productivity, and good morale. The accountability for this now sits with the *scrum master* role (or its equivalent).

Transparency and monitoring progress

The primary measure of progress on agile projects is the delivery of a working product, which reduces the overhead of formal project monitoring, especially when openly available (e.g. via dashboards).

Although the *team* update the status of their own work as they do it and the *product owner* keeps stakeholders informed, any formal reporting is still likely be a *project manager* responsibility.

Early and continual delivery of value

Although the full business benefits are often not realized until after a project has finished, real impact comes from the *team* incrementally delivering results that build toward those outcomes.

Just enough process and oversight

By delivering incrementally, the *team* build up the trust to be self-organizing. While this reduces the overhead of compliance, where required responsibility would still be with the *project manager*.

Building confidence in an uncertain world

As the only thing certain is that things will change, the whole *team* have a collective responsibility to identify and mitigate risk; however, this is still a primary *project manager* responsibility.

Planning

On agile projects, plans start at a high level and are progressively detailed as work progresses. Although the *product owner* and *team* are responsible for distinct aspects of this, overall responsibility is still primarily with the *project manager*.

The product owner should sit with the team to ensure open communication.

The scrum master role may be filled part-time by a team member, a good team leader, or an experienced agile project manager.

Stakeholder involvement

The active involvement of stakeholders is critical to the success of any project, and the collaborative nature of agile projects means that those defining the requirements are able to work alongside those delivering the solution. This enables stakeholders to see work in progress and the team to respond quickly, avoiding a formal process for requesting and approving any changes.

Business commitment
The project needs buy-in from stakeholders for adopting an agile approach, as earlier deliveries will not satisfy all requirements. It should, however, include all of the top-priority requirements and as many of the lower-priority requirements as can be included.

Stakeholders need to provide the required funding, people, and other resources. They also need to empower the team to be self-organizing around detailed decisions on requirements, priorities, and solution design.

Business needs
During the initiation stage, the project manager needs to work closely with the product owner (where present) and key stakeholders to fully understand the vision and needs. Obtaining agreement on these is crucial, as every decision made during the project should be aligned with delivering the required outcomes.

Prioritization
Stakeholders must be fully involved in defining their requirements and continually refining and prioritizing these for each delivery. As it is likely that priorities and requirements will change while the project is underway, there needs to be a mix of higher- and lower-priority requirements to give the team enough flexibility to cope with these changes. This ensures that stakeholders can absorb the impact of introducing new requirements by deprioritizing some of what they had requested.

Project sponsor
The most senior stakeholder is the project sponsor. They are the owner of the business case (the justification for the project) and they must be fully supportive of the approach being taken by the project team. They should be ready to champion the project with the rest of the organization, and be sufficiently senior with enough influence to help remove obstacles and fix problems that the project might encounter once underway.

Hot tip

Make sure the vision and needs of the business are clearly stated and understood by all.

Subject-matter experts

All subject-matter experts – both business and technical – assigned to work with the project are critical to the success of the project. Through continual feedback, they help guide development toward the required business solution. They therefore need to have the knowledge, desire, responsibility, and sufficient authority to ensure that the solution developed meets the business needs.

Communication

It is critical that all team members, whether technical or business, are able to communicate effectively with one another and any external parties. Keeping the size of the team small enough is a tremendous aid to the communication process.

Having the team located together is an ideal. However, many teams are geographically dispersed and increasingly working from home. For this reason, it is even more important to provide regular opportunities to synchronize and catch up, such as the daily stand-up meetings seen in many agile frameworks.

Team size

Larger project teams lead to increased communications effort and more formal approaches to communication, so the ideal size for an agile team is thought to be between three and nine people. On larger projects, communications and effectiveness within teams will be greatly improved by getting agreement to form multiple smaller, self-sufficient sub-teams.

While each team will be more effective, there is – however – an overhead in orchestrating work outputs from multiple teams, as this increases technical and organization change dependencies.

Tools and practices

Projects with many teams have a greater dependency on good practice and tools and communication, especially when they are dispersed over many sites. The use of video-conferencing for events like the daily stand-up will help, as will persistent chat tools that help maintain contact throughout the working day.

There has also been a huge growth in tools that support digital whiteboards for workshops and screen sharing for testing. Getting the team together for workshops like the **quarterly review and planning** event will also help team cohesion and morale.

The larger the team, the greater the need for good communication but the harder it gets.

This is also the basis for how large projects can be handled more effectively by multiple smaller teams.

High-performing teams

In an agile project, the team are self-organizing and do not require the more traditional top-down form of project management. In a small close-working team, every team member should have a good understanding of what is going on. The table below illustrates which changes in team culture can be expected:

Comparison of team culture	
High-performing agile team	Traditional team
● Shared mission	● Personal goals
● Concentrates on solutions	● Focuses on to-do lists
● Takes initiative	● Risk-averse
● Self-organizing	● Directed by others
● Joint responsibility	● Individual accountability
● Focuses on collaboration	● Motivated by reward
● Actively resolves tension	● Avoids conflict
● Looks for ways to improve	● Follows processes
● Pride in work	● Quick and dirty

Motivating the team

In place of the more traditional **command and control** role, where the project manager is expected to assign work to team members, there is a greater focus on the team's motivation and wellbeing. Thanks to rapid progress and continual feedback, most teams are able to motivate themselves; however, when any problems occur, the project manager must be prepared to help as necessary.

As a full cross-functional agile team consists of technical and business operational roles working closely together, the project manager needs to ensure they collaborate and communicate well.

Project managers who are new to leading agile projects will need to develop their style toward empowering the team, and spend more time and thought on communication with the team and with each individual team member as well.

Don't forget

On many agile projects – particularly those using the *Scrum* delivery framework – helping the team improve is the responsibility of the scrum master.

Fostering self-organization toward higher performance

The following steps will help with creating an environment where the team can thrive and develop toward higher performance:

 1 Support the team being clear on their objectives and then empower them to achieve those objectives, rather than directing the team on how they should do their work.

2 Encourage technical and business operational members of the team to collaborate actively on their work.

3 Ensure the team frequently review their progress, and watch out for non-attendance at the daily stand-up.

4 Support the team's focus by ensuring that work only comes into the team via one route – normally the product backlog as overseen by the product owner.

5 Endeavor to keep distractions and interruptions away from the team; this helps them focus on completing the work they have agreed to do.

6 Well-facilitated workshops are an excellent way of building team cohesion, providing the opportunity to collaborate on specific topics and use their combined skills to solve problems and find innovative solutions.

7 Minimize the degree of team members being swapped in and out, ideally keeping significant change to once per quarter; this protects team cohesion and performance.

8 Provide time, and funding where required, for the team to take time out together to recognize their progress and celebrate achievements.

While high performance and self-organization are not guaranteed, teams that work in environments where they feel psychologically safe and supported are more likely to evolve rapidly through the stages of forming, storming, and norming, to performing.

Hot tip

Allow time for teams to work through the Tuckman's *Stages of Team Development.*

Project life-cycles

A project life-cycle describes the stages through which a project progresses. The number and type of stages vary by approach, and the two most common archetypes are illustrated below.

Sequential project life-cycles

The focus of creating detailed plans at the outset led to the term **plan-driven** to describe these more traditional project life-cycles.

These sequential stages are based on the *Project Management Institute's* standard process groups.

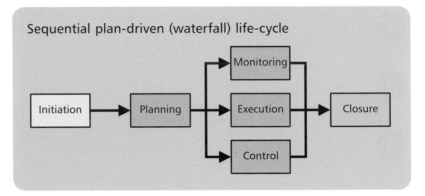

Sequential plan-driven (waterfall) life-cycle

Initiation → Planning → Monitoring / Execution / Control → Closure

Iterative project life-cycles

In order to deliver increments of value more often, agile projects need to follow a more iterative approach, with **initiation** followed by multiple cycles (iterations) of **discovery**, **delivery**, and **learning**.

These iterative stages act as a reference model for the rest of this book.

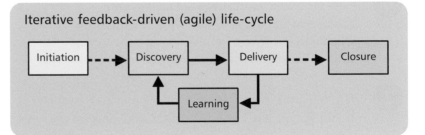

Iterative feedback-driven (agile) life-cycle

Initiation --→ Discovery → Delivery --→ Closure / Learning

The stages of this life-cycle are explored in the following chapters:

- Chapter 3: **Starting with good foundations**
- Chapter 4: **Discovery and prioritization**
- Chapter 5: **Delivering for impact**
- Chapter 6: **Transparency and learning**
- Chapter 7: **Project closure**

To achieve success through feedback-driven development, the project needs to understand and follow a blend of good practice.

Cycling back through development stages

The simplest approach to incorporate feedback would be to repeat as necessary the stages of analysis, design, programming, testing, and integration. Teams should actively pursue feedback from their stakeholders as they go, and if they find they have misunderstood anything, cycle back to the appropriate earlier stage to fix it. However, while this encourages use of feedback, it treats this as an exception rather than something that should be built in.

Iterative design

Iterative design is a deliberately cyclical process of prototyping, testing, analyzing, and refining a product design. Changes are made to the most recent iteration of a design, based on feedback. With iterative design, feedback is expected, and repeating the whole cycle is assumed.

In early cycles, there may be a greater concentration on analysis and design with a small amount of programming to generate feedback. As work progresses, understanding of the product will stabilize so that instead of reworking the analysis or design, more time is dedicated to programming and testing.

Incremental development

Incremental development is a progressive process where the product is built one feature at a time (designed, built, and tested incrementally) until it is finished. In effect, the product is broken down into its component features, each of which is developed and delivered separately. This allows the earlier release of some features, which should speed up return on investment (ROI).

Iterative design with incremental development

In order for product development to be truly feedback-driven, it is essential that the product is released progressively and repeatedly. Each release should be complete and usable, each one adding more functionality until the product is complete.

For this to be effective, you need to prioritize features so that the most useful and valuable ones are developed first. Features must be decomposed into small increments that can be delivered separately.

The principle of
last responsible moment
helps retain flexibility.
It should be noted that
for high-risk items, the
last responsible moment
could be in the very first
iteration.

Agile planning

While responding to change is valued more than following a plan,
planning is still vital on agile projects (see page 14). Rather
than making detailed commitments up-front, agile projects leave
commitment to the *last responsible moment* – planning iteratively
and incrementally at each and every level of development.

The planning onion

Planning starts during the initiation stage, with defining a vision
and identifying the scope of organization capabilities affected,
and the first-cut of potential features, as well as potential risks
and dependencies. From this, the product owner will group those
features into **minimum marketable feature** sets, and roughly plot
this along a timeline as a product roadmap.

Ongoing discovery, refinement, and planning continues alongside
product delivery, breaking the work required on larger blocks
of capability down to form their high-level product backlog,
confirming the features for each release, selecting items from the
product backlog for each iteration, and potentially replanning in
the daily stand-up to ensure the team will meet their commitment
to deliver a potentially shippable product increment each iteration.

These five levels of planning are reflected in a diagram known as
the **planning onion**, due to its arrangement of concentric circles.

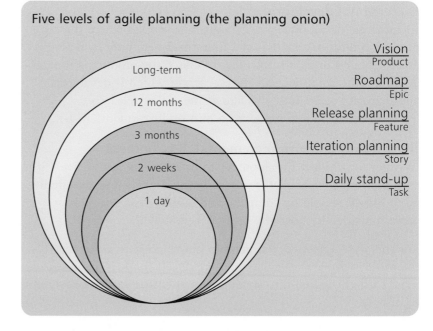

Five levels of agile planning (the planning onion)

Vision
Product
Long-term
Roadmap
Epic
12 months
Release planning
Feature
3 months
Iteration planning
Story
2 weeks
Daily stand-up
Task
1 day

The product backlog

The product backlog is equivalent to a prioritized requirements list for the project, and should be the only source of work for the team. Rather than defining all the detail up-front, the product backlog starts out as a high-level list of required capabilities, and becomes more detailed as more is known.

Priority order

The order of items on the product backlog indicates the sequence in which they will be done. The closer an item is to the top of the product backlog, the more likely it is to be implemented soon.

Items to be worked on in the near future should be detailed and narrow in scope (usually known as **stories**), while those further away will likely be more abstract and broader (known as **epics**).

Backlog refinement

Backlog refinement is an ongoing process where the product owner and the team collaborate on getting product backlog items ready, adding detail, updating assessments, and reprioritizing.

When customers can actively use the product and provide feedback, this could result in more items being added to the product backlog. As business needs or market conditions change, the product backlog will continue to evolve.

A good backlog is DEEP

This combination of factors has led to the DEEP acronym, describing a backlog that is in a good state.

- **Detailed**: Items must be detailed enough to work on, but can be more abstract the further off they are from being done.

- **Estimated**: The team must have had the opportunity to review planned work to consider solution options and assess the complexity, risk, and effort (see Chapter 4).

- **Emergent**: Items can be added and removed at any point, and during refinement larger items will be decomposed into several smaller items (some of which may not get done).

- **Prioritized**: Items should be prioritized to indicate business value, urgency, and dependency sequencing; prioritizing any items higher should lead to other items moving down the list.

Managing risk and uncertainty

As mentioned earlier, the only thing certain on agile projects is that things will change. Our choice to follow an agile approach is precisely because the degree of uncertainty is higher. By limiting commitments to the shorter term we keep more options open, making it easier to adapt when we do encounter problems.

Risks and impediments

Anything that can slow teams down or block them from completing their work is classed as an **impediment** (the term used on agile projects for *issues*). These might be potential (i.e. risks) or actual (i.e. already occurred).

As soon as an impediment or risk is identified, the team should actively manage it by capturing it, assessing it, agreeing how to respond, and continuing to monitor it until it has passed. The aim of risk management is to stop it from becoming an impediment or to minimize its impact should that occur.

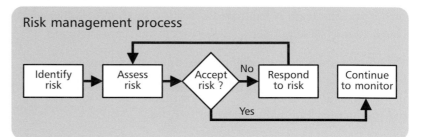

Identifying risks and impediments

Whoever identifies a risk or impediment should capture a short description, along with anything else that is helpful. This is typically on a RAID card, displayed on the team board or project risk board.

The acronym *RAID* covers *risks* and *impediments,* as well as *assumptions* and *dependencies* (two other common types of risk).

Assessing risks and impediments

The team should next assess the potential impact and likelihood, along with the date by which it might become critical. Assessment is typically on a 1-5 scale. For likelihood, this represents a range from unlikely through to it having already occurred. For impact, this ranges from minimal to severe. A combined risk score should then be calculated by multiplying the assessments for impact and likelihood. Any risk score in the range 1-6 would be low risk, 7-14 medium risk, and 15 or above should be considered high risk.

For example: It is highly likely that the team brought together for the Outage Reporter at **Vanguard Power** would underestimate the work required in their first few iterations, but the impact is lower as they have time to make it up. Whereas, as they improve, the likelihood of them underestimating diminishes, but if it happens right at the end, the impact would be much higher.

Responding to risks and impediments

Once the team have assessed the impact and likelihood, they should decide what response to make and who owns that. Responses typically include *resolution*, *mitigation*, or *acceptance*. In mitigating a risk or impediment, the team will take steps to reduce its impact or likelihood. In resolving it, the team will fix or remove the underlying problem. In accepting it, the team have agreed that they can live with the implications.

For anything that is high-impact and highly likely or already happened, the team should take action immediately. If the team do not have the capacity or capability to resolve the risk or impediment, it should be escalated (see page 37).

Monitoring risks and impediments

The ongoing status of any risks, assumptions, impediments, or dependencies should be tracked and reviewed regularly. If either likelihood or impact increases or decreases, this should trigger a reassessment. Finally, it can be closed off when it has been resolved, its potential impact date has passed, or the combined risk score has become so low it is no longer a concern.

Teams could review this at their daily stand-up or similar project level event. An assessment of overall risk level and any changes should be shared with stakeholders in iteration reviews, and assessed in team retrospectives for opportunities to improve.

Establishing transparency

To be effective, all agile project management and delivery frameworks are based on the principles of empirical thinking: transparency, inspection, and adaptation.

Transparency
High-performing agile teams invest time when they form to establish a **working agreement** of the behaviors, practices, and standards they want to work by. Once underway, they also ensure that their progress is easily visible to each other and their stakeholders. Transparency is a cornerstone of good agile practice.

Inspection
The team should pause regularly to review the work they've produced and how well they have been working, taking an evidence-based approach by using objective metrics.

Adaptation
When the results of a product review or team retrospective highlight an opportunity to improve, the team should add it to the product backlog so that it is considered alongside other work.

Communication plan
To maximize the impact of this transparency, it's critical that everyone with a vested interest in the project's outcomes is actively engaged in two-way communication (rather than only being the recipients of project updates and announcements). The communication plan should include all key stakeholders, what their interest would be, along with method and frequency.

Communicating with the sponsor
The most senior stakeholder is the project sponsor. They are responsible for the business case and budget, and must have enough influence to be able to resolve business issues and make financial decisions where required. It is critical to keep them particularly engaged and informed, ensuring they have access to view real-time progress and inviting them to reviews.

Communicating within the project team
Team meetings are very effective for real-time communication; however, to help the team focus on delivery, keep in-person meetings for when two-way dialog is really required, such as in decision-making workshops. For one-way communication, it is better to use information radiators, such as whiteboards or charts.

Don't forget

This continual inspection and adaptation takes the place of more formal monitoring and control.

Monitoring and reporting

On plan-driven projects, progress is often tracked against a detailed project plan on a Gantt chart. On agile projects, there are typically many activities going on in parallel, and a different approach to progress monitoring is therefore required. Options include progress on completing scope for a release or within individual iterations.

Release burn-up chart

For each release, typically quarterly, the team will estimate the features they forecast can be delivered in each iteration. This is charted on the release burn-up, which compares work progressively delivered against forecast through the quarter.

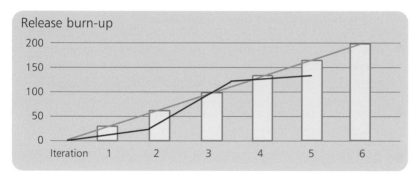

Release burn-up

A template for a burn-up chart is provided on our website. Go to https://ineasysteps.com/downloads/

The iteration burn-down chart (see page 87) fulfills a similar role within a single iteration, and tends to be used solely by the team.

Timesheets

While never popular, many organizations still calculate assets on the basis of time and money spent, meaning projects need all team members to record the time they spend by deliverable. Ideally this can be dispensed with, but where necessary it should be recorded automatically by their product backlog management tool.

However it is done, keeping records of actuals against forecast helps significantly to improve future estimates.

Escalation procedure

When impediments occur they should be handled at the lowest appropriate level. Ideally, the affected team should resolve everything where possible. However, if it is outside their scope, it should be escalated to the project level, normally immediately after the team's daily stand-up.

For organization impediments or decisions requiring higher levels of authority, the project manager would then escalate it to the project sponsor, and so on, up the executive team if required.

Never hide issues and risk springing a surprise on the project sponsor!

Summary

- The linear and sequential nature of traditional project management approaches makes them increasingly unsuited to the many challenges that organizations face today.

- Iterative and incremental approaches are three times more likely to lead to project success, as well as three times less likely to fail.

- The two biggest indicators of project success are the size of commitment combined with adapting based on feedback.

- The project manager role has evolved more toward leadership than management, with many of the traditional accountabilities taken on by other roles.

- The agile approach to project management focuses on the empowerment of the team, less formal progress monitoring, team motivation, and the full involvement of the business.

- Active and ongoing stakeholder engagement is critical to successful outcomes.

- Agile teams need enough stability and commitment to deliver to enable self-organization, productivity, and good morale.

- The agile approach needs to allow for regular opportunities to pause and review the product developed, and reflect on performance and adapt their approach where necessary.

- Rather than full planning up-front, agile planning starts at a high level with the detail progressively elaborated throughout.

- Agile project management frameworks are more lightweight, freeing up more time to focus on delivery.

- By developing in small increments, teams are able to deliver selected outcomes earlier and generate more feedback to ensure requirements are met.

- The formality of monitoring and control is reduced, with increased transparency of progress combined with the frequency of joint reviews and retrospectives.

- By limiting the size of commitment and delivering more frequently, agile projects are more resilient to the heightened risks and uncertainties in complex and novel projects.

3 Starting with good foundations

You only start a project once, so it is worth doing it well. This chapter covers activities in iteration zero – before we get started – when we determine the feasibility and set strong foundations for the stages that follow.

Foundations for success

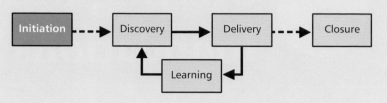

Agile project management life-cycle

Initiation ---▶ Discovery ▶ Delivery ---▶ Closure

Learning

Known in some agile frameworks as **inception**, **start-up**, and as **sprint zero** or **iteration zero** (i.e. before delivery starts), the primary purpose of the **initiation** stage is to set the project up to succeed. Always required when starting a new project or forming a new team, it is also a useful exercise for teams that stay together at the end of their project and need to re-establish their foundations and find a new purpose.

It can be tempting to rush to start the repeating loop of discovery, delivery, and learning as quickly as possible, but as the saying goes, "*you only get one opportunity to make a first impression*". It is therefore critical to strike a balance, keeping the initiation stage relatively short while investing just enough time to:

- Establish objectives and vision.

- Ensure alignment with strategy.

- Form the team.

- Agree on the team's working practices.

- Draft an initial plan.

- Justify the initial funding to get started.

Continued foundations
One of the additional benefits of agile project management is the potential of ending a project earlier than planned, typically when enough value has been delivered and any further value is less than may be gained from investing in an alternative project.

Agile portfolio management and **Lean Governance** approaches will actively reconsider a project's justification throughout its life-cycle when they review the project's progress or consider their overall portfolio of work against a pipeline of potential new projects.

Don't forget

Initial scoping and solutioning is often conducted alongside the initiation stage; however, as these are ongoing activities on agile projects, they are covered more fully in Chapter 4.

Design-thinking for projects

Borrowing from the product management world, the approach of design-thinking suggests that the ideal product or project comes at the junction of what is desirable, feasible, and viable.

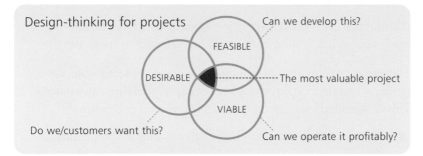

- **Desirable**: To be considered, any project should contribute to an organization's goals and be something that their stakeholders and customers would consider valuable.

- **Feasible**: Assuming a project is desirable, an organization needs to determine whether this is something they are able to develop by themselves, buy in, or partner with someone else.

- **Viable**: Even when a project is both desirable and feasible, an organization still needs to consider the organizational change implications of any process redesign, organization restructuring, hiring, and training that might be required.

Provided the project can be demonstrated as desirable, feasible, and viable, it then needs to be prioritized against all other potential projects in the portfolio.

Portfolio pipeline forum

Vanguard Power – the fictitious energy business used to illustrate key points – have a **portfolio pipeline forum**, made up of key representatives from all operational and corporate business units. The group was established to ensure transparency, objectivity, and sound governance, ensuring everyone understands the impact of their decisions and that they can compete fairly for a limited budget.

They meet fortnightly, to review progress on in-flight projects, consider new project proposals, and act as a point of escalation and guidance for any dependencies, risks, and impediments that might be blocking a project.

Communicating the vision

To start with good foundations we need a clear vision and purpose for bringing a team together. There are never enough people or funds for all the work our organizations would like to do, so the vision needs to be sufficiently compelling to our stakeholders for this to be prioritized against other potential work.

Although a draft vision may have been drafted by the sponsor to reach this point, it now needs to be developed in more detail.

The project vision should briefly lay out the project's objectives, scope, schedule, budget, risks, and other supporting information. This is foundational for the project for several reasons:

Hot tip

A project vision is similar to the more traditional *terms of reference*, although it should be 1-2 pages.

- It summarizes what has been agreed during the **initiation** stage.

- Stakeholders understand the expected outcomes.

- The team will be clear on their purpose.

- The project will have enough shape to be considered.

Project vision

The following is an example of a project vision for **Vanguard Power**. They have decided to develop services to help consumers report power outages.

Project vision
For power consumers frustrated and anxious during network outages, the *Outage Reporter* will be an application that enables consumers to report new outages and faults in our network, and to monitor progress on any that have already been reported.

Project objectives
The combination of a growing population and more extreme weather patterns has led to an increase in power outages and faults in the last 18 months. Our market reputation has suffered and we have had to pay penalties to the industry regulator.

The goal for this project is to provide consumers with the ability to report power outages faster and to see outages already reported with what is being done.

Sponsor is Chief Networks Officer, William Watts.

Outline scope
The proposal is to kick off discovery to confirm requirements, solution options, and feasibility, with the aim of launching a service to consumers within six months.

Dependencies and constraints
The project requires third-party support to integrate this application with the Network Operations Management System (NOMS).

Team requirements
We need a team to conduct the discovery and then begin delivery of the initial proof of concept. Feasibility will take two iterations and completion a further eight iterations (i.e. under six months).

Funding required
Forecast based on standard team costs of $50K per iteration:

Feasibility: $100K
Completion: $400K

Creating alignment

To be confident in gaining approval, project foundations describe how the project will reflect and contribute to the organization's strategy and direction, both business and technical.

Creating alignment helps ensure that the team will be doing the right thing and that they will be doing it the right way. It should also improve consistency, quality, and speed of delivery by taking advantage of guidelines, templates, and existing assets.

The reuse of existing assets is particularly advantageous, as it not only demonstrates continuing value from those assets, but also provides more capacity for the team to focus on adding new value.

Key considerations for alignment

- Roadmaps for strategy, operations, staffing, and technology.

- Standards and guidelines for architecture, branding, coding, documentation, risk management, security, tools, usability, etc.

- Any templates that should be adopted.

- Any enterprise assets that should be reused, such as services, tools, frameworks, components, etc.

- Governance strategies to be followed, such as security, release management, quality, finance, etc.

This should help shine a light onto an organization's governance processes and influence leadership toward leaner governance.

Alignment at Vanguard Power

There was already concern in **Vanguard Power**'s executive team regarding the recent bad press, as well as the fines. The objectives demonstrated how this work would help address those concerns, as well as aligning to the strategic need to guarantee network uptime.

The project vision also showed the intention of integrating this application with their Network Operations Management System (NOMS). As well as addressing their short-term concerns, the executive team could also see how this would enable the network operations team to be alerted sooner and help highlight areas getting multiple notifications closely together. Although this would require additional work outside the scope of this project, this was accepted as being the subject of a separate project proposal, as it would likely need to be completed by a separate team as well.

Forming the team

A key part of the initiation stage is to identify and form a team so that they are available and ready to start discovery as soon as approval is gained.

Although membership of the team might evolve as more is understood, the project needs sufficient people to support initial discovery during initiation.

There will be some key decisions to make during initiation, across areas such as scope, schedule, solution options, and development approach. An underlying principle of agile delivery is that these types of decisions should be made by those doing the work, so forming the team earlier avoids a decision-making bottleneck.

Factors for forming teams

A good team needs the right mix of people, with the right skills and an open mindset, combined with a willingness to collaborate and learn together. This also needs to be supported by fostering the right environment for them to focus and work unimpeded.

Additional team-formation factors include where members will be drawn from, where they will be located, and whether the organization is willing to commit them to full-time teams.

It is not uncommon for team members to retain some operational responsibilities alongside any shared purpose in joining a project team. While it would be better for them to bring all their responsibilities into the team, this can work so long as the team are clear on their available capacity.

Some consideration should also be given to how team improvement will be facilitated, whether by a member of the team, a separate team coach, or a more experienced mentor.

Vanguard Power's Outage Reporter team

The costs in **Vanguard Power**'s project vision (see page 42) were for an average-sized team of seven to eight people. However, to get things going during initiation, Vanguard agreed to form a discovery team (see page 52). This consisted of a business analyst, a senior app developer, a backend systems specialist, and a user-experience designer. They were supported by the project manager and a key representative from the risk management team (who would act as their equivalent of a product owner). They agreed to wait until the early discovery was completed to confirm who else they needed.

Beware

Avoid splitting people between multiple teams, as this creates too much context-switching and results in loss of focus.

Agreeing on working practices

Most organizations will have standards and guidelines for a range of project deliverables and activities, and alignment with these was discussed in the preceding pages. Once the team are formed, one of their first activities should be to consider the working practices they will follow.

This is best conducted as a workshop with an experienced facilitator, who will ensure all team members are fully involved.

Collaborating on working practices commonly helps a team to:

- Understand each other's respective skills and goals.

- Decide which regular meetings or events they need to book to ensure they continually plan, work, review, and improve.

- Agree on basic meeting etiquette, such as: clear agendas, starting promptly, no phones, and capturing actions.

- Establish decision-making protocols, such as whether key decisions have to be by consensus, majority, or advisory.

- Sign up to collective ownership of the team's outcomes, alongside the individual responsibilities of their discipline.

- Commit to building in quality and excellence, rather than checking after the fact.

- Acknowledge the processes they must follow, and identify where they might need to deviate so that they can negotiate that.

- Set an example for how they should communicate and collaborate throughout their time together.

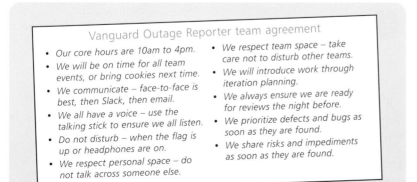

Vanguard Outage Reporter team agreement

- Our core hours are 10am to 4pm.
- We will be on time for all team events, or bring cookies next time.
- We communicate – face-to-face is best, then Slack, then email.
- We all have a voice – use the talking stick to ensure we all listen.
- Do not disturb – when the flag is up or headphones are on.
- We respect personal space – do not talk across someone else.
- We respect team space – take care not to disturb other teams.
- We will introduce work through iteration planning.
- We always ensure we are ready for reviews the night before.
- We prioritize defects and bugs as soon as they are found.
- We share risks and impediments as soon as they are found.

Some project frameworks have separate *feasibility* and *foundations* stages, but they are increasingly completed together.

46

Assessing feasibility

The purpose of a feasibility assessment is to establish whether or not any proposed work is technically feasible and viable from a business perspective – and if there are any realistic alternatives.

On some projects, especially larger ones, feasibility may be run as a separate stage, in which case, the primary outputs would be a feasibility assessment (see the example on the opposite page) and an outline plan. However, this is increasingly seen as part of the foundations activity required to initiate all agile projects.

Objectives

The following are the main objectives of assessing feasibility, and the steps that will need to be completed to achieve them:

1 Explore whether or not there is a solution to the scope, as described in the project vision.

2 Identify any possible alternative options that would meet the requirements.

3 Validate the high-level business benefits that are likely to follow each option.

4 Confirm whether each solution could be delivered within current capabilities, or whether changes would be required.

5 Consider the operational impact of each option, to avoid going with an option that looks cheaper to deliver but that would drive a higher total cost of ownership.

6 Recommend which option would best meet longer-term interests, while still being achievable within reasonable time and budgetary constraints.

The time committed to assessing feasibility should be kept as light as possible, as the main purpose is to establish whether or not it is worth proceeding with.

There will be further exploration of scope and solution options during discovery, which might necessitate reviewing the assumptions and decisions made during initiation (see Chapter 4).

Although it is useful to assess feasibility during the initiation stage, it should be reviewed whenever significant new scope is uncovered during discovery.

Feasibility assessment

As the key deliverable from this stage, the feasibility assessment extends the project vision with: an assessment of the business impact, the technical feasibility, and the business viability of any options considered. It should also include any additional considerations of note.

Outage Reporter Feasibility Assessment:

#	Option	Desirability	Feasibility	Viability	Assessment
A	Do nothing	Does not address concerns with regulator or reputation	N/A	N/A	Least preferred
B	Stand-alone web app	Consumer-facing, though requires a device with a browser	Already have skilled and experienced staff	Resolves the issues. Increases call center workload	Good candidate. Least cost
C	Stand-alone smartphone app	Consumer-facing	Can readily hire both Apple and Android developers	(as for option B)	Good candidate. Higher cost than B
D	Integrate app with NOMS (B or C)	Enables faster response times	Past experience of integrating with NOMS	Resolves the issues. Improves effectiveness for network operations	Best candidate. Highest cost

Primary deliverable

This project will deliver a consumer-facing app for reporting outages that we could develop as a website (B) or a smartphone app (C). We have a good track record with web development, and can hire app developers with Apple or Android experience.

Additional deliverables

(D) Integrating this with the Network Operations Management System (NOMS) will allow us to respond to outages much sooner. We have previously integrated our call center systems with NOMS.

Recommended approach

While the options to develop a stand-alone web or smartphone app would meet the objectives, and are cheaper, they would drive more work into the call center. However, the recommended approach is to develop and deploy to address the concerns, and then enhance with integration to NOMS. Although that drives increased workload into the call center, that is in the short term only, and we could improve how consumers report outages based on call center experience.

Additional considerations

While the integration would require support from our vendor, they have agreed to support this at no cost for rights to intellectual property.

Outlining the initial plan

On agile projects, planning is also done iteratively and incrementally, getting progressively more detailed. At the highest level, planning starts with the vision, and detailed commitments are left to the *last responsible moment* (see page 32).

Early discovery uncovers features and maps them onto a roadmap. Ongoing discovery continues finding features for each release, confirming items for each iteration, and replanning each day.

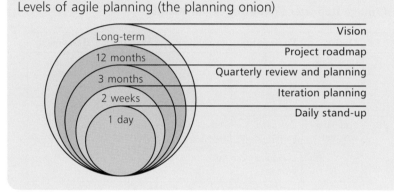

Levels of agile planning (the planning onion)

Long-term	Vision
12 months	Project roadmap
3 months	Quarterly review and planning
2 weeks	Iteration planning
1 day	Daily stand-up

As the team collaborate on the initial plan, they can guide stakeholders about what is achievable within a certain time or budget. This can also help stakeholders improve their agile mindset by realizing earlier that they should look at alternatives.

Factors of planning for initiation

The team should consider the following factors in how they will work together (many are explored further in Chapter 4):

- **Involved**: The team, product owner, domain experts, leadership.

- **Scope**: The whole product or just the next release increment.

- **Scheduling**: Continual flow, incremental, scope- or date-driven.

- **Timeline**: Rolling wave, quarterly, biweekly, or alternative.

- **Estimating**: Educated guess, relative estimation, planning poker, function points, even no estimates (see the Hot tip).

- **Estimates**: Order of magnitude, T-shirt sizes, story points.

- **Format**: Quarterly roadmap, iteration schedule, release burn-down, or more traditional forms such as a Gantt chart.

Hot tip

High-performing teams may reach a point where they don't need to estimate individual items. Not for the faint-hearted or inexperienced.

Approval and funding

The funding for the initiation stage is typically sourced from an organization's portfolio management capability. So as initiation draws to a conclusion, additional funds will need to be justified based on the vision and outline plan to continue with discovery, complete team formation, and get started on delivery.

In larger organizations, funding approvals and portfolio management are likely to spread across multiple functions, teams, and forums. This can make approval and funding to continue a drawn-out process, so good preparation is essential for success.

Smaller organizations might benefit from these activities being governed by a single team – this can often be more dependent on who you know. In these cases, it can be even more critical to engage and share the vision with the right stakeholders early on.

Funding choices

Either way, the team should have considered these choices:

- **Cadence**: Will funding be needed entirely in advance, for the quarter, by iteration, or potentially continual?

- **Access**: Will funding be drawn down as needed against an approved pool, requested by the agreed cadence, or treated as operational expenditure?

- **Team basis**: Will the team be needed just for the duration of the project, long-term to support a specific product or line of business, or even established as a value stream profit center?

As fixed-price funding is often considered the riskiest option, organizations have been considering options such as stable funding of value streams rather than project-based funding.

Funding decision

At **Vanguard Power**, the early discovery has confirmed that the scope outlined in the vision is achievable within six months, and should reduce the severity of future outages. As recent penalties for badly-handled outages ranged between three to five million dollars, the investment of half a million dollars was easily justified.

With a rare outbreak of agreement, the portfolio pipeline forum approved funding for a team for 12 months, in the expectation that further ideas would be discovered as work progressed.

Summary

- Avoid the temptation to rush into delivery by taking just enough time to set up the project for success.

- Validate that there is a good business case for the work, and that it is desirable, technically feasible, and viable to be operated.

- Develop a vision for the project – traditionally known as the *terms of reference* – that also captures the objectives, likely scope, any known dependencies or constraints, teaming and funding requirements.

- Ensure alignment with business and technical strategy.

- Form a good cross-functional team with all the skills the team will need to deliver a quality working product.

- Within the organization's standard and guidelines, facilitate the new team to determine their working practices and form a team agreement – sometimes called a *social contract*.

- Assess the technical and business feasibility and viability of a number of potential solution options that could meet the remit of the project.

- Document the feasibility assessment, showing which options were considered, how well each met the criteria, and what your recommendations are.

- Planning happens differently on agile projects, with early high-level work on a vision and roadmap and detailed planning left closer to when the work will be done – often in a quarterly review and planning cycle, and then each iteration (typically two weeks), and then refreshed on a daily basis.

- Decide on the best approach to funding the work, which could be based on quarterly funding, drawing down when needed, or funding the team for the whole duration.

- Gain funding approval for the next stage, to complete more discovery and start delivery.

- It is worth noting that most projects will conduct some high-level discovery in parallel with initiating the project – these activities are covered in Chapter 4.

4 Discovery and prioritization

The team need to start by defining the work they intend to do, and continue doing this in parallel with delivery and learning. This chapter explores how work is discovered, defined, prioritized, and estimated.

Discovery

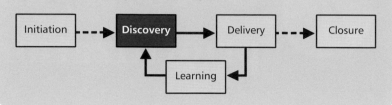

Agile project management life-cycle

Initiation ---> **Discovery** ---> Delivery ---> Closure

Learning

Rather than starting out with a solution in mind, successful project teams break the overall work into smaller more frequent deliverables (see Chapter 2) so that they are able to discover and define scope as they go and elicit feedback that helps refine that.

This is depicted by the repeating loop of **discovery**, **delivery**, and **learning** in the generic life-cycle (illustrated above).

Before starting this cycle, the project team will have undertaken some discovery as part of **initiation** (see Chapter 3), to ensure they understand the goals their stakeholders are looking to achieve and whether they can deliver a solution that helps achieve those goals.

Once underway, the project team should continue to seek out and clarify scope at a high level, as well as refining and improving the definition of what has already been identified.

Discovery team

Many agile projects form a **discovery team** for this, known as the *product team* in some organizations. While this often consists of a product owner, business analyst, and user-experience designer, it should strive to be representative of all perspectives:

- Stakeholders and customers, to represent and help clarify what is necessary and desirable.

- Change managers and operational roles, to represent what would be required for a solution to be operationally viable.

- Technical roles, such as architects, to represent what would be required for a solution to be technically feasible to deliver.

- Depending on context, the discovery team could also call on subject-matter experts such as market research and prototyping (to help with very novel products) or finance and legal counsel (to clarify complex business rules).

Don't forget

Although the life-cycle depicts the stages of discovery, delivery, and learning as sequential, they are really happening at the same time.

52

Hot tip

Some organizations involve the whole project team in discovery, but most will limit this to representatives, to help the rest of the team stay focused on delivery.

Discovery workshops

The discovery team will usually work through facilitated workshops to understand the needs of their customers and stakeholders, and potential solutions. These workshops will help the discovery team to define the work sufficiently that an experienced project team can then design and deliver a viable solution from the very first iteration.

Project advisory group

As a group representative of many key stakeholders, a discovery team can sometimes also act as an advisory or supervisory group for the project. In this mode, they will tend to meet on a more regular basis (as often as once or twice per week), and in addition to discussing new work, their agenda will also include a progress review, requests for clarification, and handling escalations.

Ongoing refinement

While the discovery team (or its equivalent) identify and describe the high-level capabilities and behaviors required, these need to be broken down and described in more detail before the project team can bring them into an iteration planning session.

This ongoing work to provide more detail is typically called **backlog refinement**, and should involve the whole project team – collaborating on getting these items ready, adding detail, updating assessments, and reprioritizing. Most teams will set aside an hour or so every single week to collaborate in a refinement workshop.

Definition of ready

To avoid any ambiguity of what the project team need in order to bring backlog items into an iteration planning session, many teams agree and capture this as their **definition of ready**, such as:

It is critical that work on agile projects is detailed and estimated by the people who will deliver them. No one else tells them how to do their work or how long it should take.

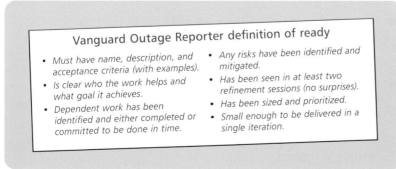

Vanguard Outage Reporter definition of ready

- *Must have name, description, and acceptance criteria (with examples).*
- *Is clear who the work helps and what goal it achieves.*
- *Dependent work has been identified and either completed or committed to be done in time.*
- *Any risks have been identified and mitigated.*
- *Has been seen in at least two refinement sessions (no surprises).*
- *Has been sized and prioritized.*
- *Small enough to be delivered in a single iteration.*

Scoping the product backlog

Eliciting and capturing the required capabilities and behaviors starts during the initiation stage and continues throughout the project. Any requirement uncovered, all feedback received, and any unexpected complexity need to go through the same steps to be assessed for desirability, feasibility, viability, and impact on scope.

Building the product backlog

As capabilities and behaviors are identified, they will be captured into the **product backlog** (the *prioritized requirements list* for all work to be completed in the project). All backlog items for the project must be in a single product backlog and should be the only source of work coming into the team.

This makes it easier to value and size backlog items relatively, allows the team to assess and communicate the impact of any changes, and avoids the team being distracted by working with more than one product owner.

The product backlog is dynamic and evolving, with backlog items starting as high-level descriptions of capabilities that are then progressively broken down and detailed as the team get ready to work on each one. High-level items are typically referred to as **epics**, while more detailed items are known as **stories**.

These will likely be supplemented with other models that capture the user experience, business processes, and overriding system-quality attributes (like performance and scalability).

Benefits of scoping

Capturing the scope in the product backlog has several benefits.

- It helps answer common stakeholder questions, especially around what will be delivered, how much it might cost, and when it might be delivered.

- It helps develop confidence in what could be done first, by doing just enough requirements elicitation to understand what stakeholders want.

- It helps set expectations as to what will be delivered, with the stakeholders working with representatives of the team to reach agreement around a scope that will deliver on the vision and can be completed within the funds the organization is willing to invest.

Backlog items

A backlog item will usually start out as just a title or high-level description. Eventually it should also have an indication of its value, how it will be validated, the likely size of the work, and any associated risks and dependencies. These will be added progressively over time, with the backlog item meeting the team's definition of ready before iteration planning.

Epics

As the highest backlog item, an **epic** is large, broadly defined, and typically describes an entire workflow. When it comes time to plan the work into iterations, it needs to be broken down.

Epics are often named with an action and an object; for example, *Notify power outages* or *Confirm power restored*.

Stories

A **story** describes a discrete part of the overall functionality, acting as a building block. Historically, stories were hand-written on index cards. Today, they are typically created and tracked in a digital agile management tool. Most tools allow stories to be printed so that the team can track them on a physical board if they choose.

A story describes functionality that enables a customer to achieve a specific job. This should be kept brief and written in everyday business language, to prompt a conversation at the time of doing the work. This is typically in the format of a **user story**.

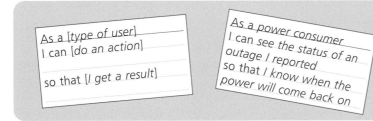

The user story would be on the front of the index card, while the acceptance criteria (see page 57) would be written on the back.

Features

For most projects, two levels of product decomposition is enough, so most teams stick with just epics and stories. However, for more work that involves multiple teams, some also use a **feature** as a planning and decomposition level between an epic and its stories.

Investing in a well-formed backlog

There is an art form to crafting backlog items that are truly fit for purpose. They need to meet the multiple needs of communicating the intent of the product owner (or equivalent), be easy to understand for the delivery team, and be flexible enough to be used for ongoing discovery and delivery.

There is a widely accepted set of criteria for what makes a backlog item well formed. Where a backlog item does not meet all of these criteria, the team may want it rewritten, rescoped, broken down, or potentially even discarded completely.

These criteria form a checklist for assessing backlog items, made memorable through the acronym of **INVEST**:

- **Independent**: The product owner should be able to move backlog items around easily to change the order in which product features will be developed – so backlog items should be reasonably independent of each other.

- **Negotiable**: A backlog item's description is necessarily brief, like the user-story format (see page 55), and requires conversation closer to the time of being developed – this allows the product owner to limit commitment to as late as is responsible and allows for changing requirements.

- **Valuable**: Every backlog item must have some discernible value, whether it is the functionality it provides the customer, the feedback and insight it will provide, or how it enables some other function – this is covered by the **so that** clause in the user-story format.

- **Estimatable**: A backlog item must be well-enough defined so that the team can consider how they might do the work and be relatively certain of the complexity, risk, and effort involved.

- **Small**: A backlog item should be sized such that a team could complete it with a few days of effort – so an epic would be too large and should be broken down (see page 65).

- **Testable**: It should be clear how the team will know when they have delivered what is required of a backlog item – the product owner needs to provide unambiguous acceptance criteria (see the next page) and the team should be able to generate testable examples to prove or disprove those.

Beware

Any story larger than a few days of effort will often have hidden risks or complexities that result in the team developing the wrong solution, taking too long, or failing to complete it.

Acceptance criteria

While the backlog item should help the team understand the goal a customer will be able to achieve, it is still not equivalent to the detailed requirements we might be used to. However, acceptance criteria do provide that next level of detail, as they should define how the product owner plans to confirm whether the work is really complete and ready for release.

Acceptance criteria are statements that define what the product must and must not do, and specify both functional requirements (e.g. how the functionality enables someone to achieve a goal) and non-functional requirements (e.g. access and authentication).

Each criterion should have a clear pass-or-fail condition; there can be no partial acceptance. They define the boundaries of the work and provide certainty to the team for when a story can be considered complete and working as required.

Well-defined acceptance criteria

The language used must be clear, helping the team understand how their work will be tested – using relatively simple terms while still providing enough precision to be useful.

Acceptance criteria must state the intent but not the solution. The phrasing should be the same, regardless of the platform the application is intended for – e.g. desktop, web, or smartphone.

Here's an example: *"Can confirm a notification is for a new outage"* rather than *"Can click the new button to add the outage to the database"*.

Types of acceptance criteria

Acceptance criteria cover everything that is important to test that a story is working as required. Typical examples include:

- **Functional**: Defines the functions the story will introduce – for example, *"Can list all known outages in my area"*.

- **Non-functional**: Defines the conditions the story must meet – for example, *"Cannot notify an outage if not authenticated"*.

- **Performance**: Where speed of response, availability, or scalability is critical to the acceptance of an individual story, it should be explicitly included – for example, *"Response time is under five seconds"*.

Outlining the solution

As the project team start to discover and build the product backlog, they should also start looking at how they will approach designing the possible solutions. During the initiation stage this focuses more on the early architectural decisions, but continues throughout the project as new work is discovered.

Evolving architecture

Just as with project planning, on agile projects the architecture is not decided completely at the start of the project. However, it is prudent to invest some time during initiation to consider the direction that the solution architecture could take. This will help guide thinking as the details evolve later.

Retiring risk early

A key benefit of considering the high-level architecture early and continuously is identifying risks – for example, uncovering technology or critical dependencies that would cause delays if discovered later. This also provides opportunities to schedule some early exploration, such as a **proof of concept** or **analysis spike**.

Avoiding technical debt

The concept of **technical debt** describes the cost of rework caused by teams adopting a workaround or wrong solution and then having to revisit and change it later. Uncovering and considering key technical decisions before the team have started defining solutions or started delivery should also reduce the amount of technical debt and rework required.

Stakeholder engagement

Although the focus of stakeholders should primarily be on the outcomes of the project, they will likely want to know how this will be achieved before starting or continuing to fund the work.

Solution outline for the Outage Reporter project

Vanguard Power want their Network Operations staff made aware when new outage and fault reports are submitted, so the project hopes to reuse the same interface implemented for their call center to report outages phoned in by members of the public.

That assumption represents a technical risk, so they have planned a proof of concept to test using the same interface. This will need support from the Network Operations Management System (NOMS) vendor, as identified in the project vision.

Exploring options

As work progresses on building the product backlog and outlining possible solutions, the wider project team will get more engaged in exploring what the detailed solution could look like.

Ready for exploration

As discussed at the start of this chapter, teams should consider having a definition of ready (see page 53) so that there is clarity of how much detail is required to commit to the work in an iteration. In a similar way, there is also a minimum criterion before teams can even explore potential options for the solution.

- Stakeholders and the portfolio management function must have accepted that the project vision provides a suitable foundation on which a solution can be developed.

- All physical, technical, and other requirements are in place and adequate to support delivery.

- All of the required roles are in place and ready to work, including those assigned to the project and any subject-matter experts who may contribute on an occasional basis.

Objectives

There are five key objectives to consider when exploring options:

1. Continue developing and elaborating the requirements established during early discovery during the initiation stage, as captured in the product backlog.

2. Explore the needs of stakeholders in more depth and develop more detailed requirements based on these needs.

3. Build a functional and demonstrable solution that satisfies these requirements.

4. Demonstrate a working solution to the stakeholders who will use, support, and maintain it.

5. Develop further the business area and system architecture definitions, and create models that illustrate how the solution will work and how it supports existing or planned business processes and systems.

Prioritizing

To meet the team's definition of ready, the product owner will typically need to order the backlog so that the work they would like considered for the next iteration is at the top. Prioritizing the backlog will be influenced by a number of criteria:

- **Business value**: The product owner must ensure the team understand the value of each item to be considered.

- **Technical debt**: Teams should prioritize anything that stops the product from working or blocks them from new work.

- **Retiring risk early**: Anything the team deem to be more uncertain or complex is worth resolving earlier – if it takes longer than expected, this doesn't come as a late surprise.

- **Clearing dependent work**: Whenever work is identified as dependent on other work, that other work must be done first.

- **Testing a hypothesis**: Where the product owner wants to test an idea or the team need to confirm their technical approach.

- **Clearing aged items**: Anything that has been a low priority for a long time should be reassessed – take it back through the discovery process or consider discarding it altogether.

Striking a balance

An early agile approach to prioritization, known as the MoSCoW method (see page 122), involves assessing each backlog item as:

- **Must have**: A mandatory need, especially for compliance.

- **Should have**: An important need, now or very soon.

- **Could have**: A nice-to-have need; do it if capacity allows.

- **Won't have**: Agreed as not a priority now, but may be in the future.

While this seems easy, classifying 80% of a backlog as *must have* does not help the team to decide when to do things. On the other hand, the team only really need to know what they are being asked to look at over the next few iterations.

The techniques on the opposite page strike a balance between over-simplification and over-thinking. The right combination will depend on your organization and team – so it is best to explore these early on and agree on a balance that works for you.

More objective prioritization

Stakeholders are often asked to force-rank backlog items based on the order in which they feel each should be built. This misses out on hidden complexities – like technical dependencies – and often leads to conflict. To avoid these challenges, adopt a more objective queueing model.

It is best to avoid conflict in prioritization – never just give way to the *highest-paid person's opinion* (the HIPPO).

- **Shortest duration first**: Prioritizing the effort alone will get some work released sooner – however, this can often be low-value work.

- **Highest value first**: Alternatively, prioritizing by potential value should lead to greater returns from the first release, but it may take a long time.

  Alongside the obvious *business value* – like revenue growth – also consider *operational value*, like improving workflow, and *time criticality*, like regulatory compliance – together, these are known as the **cost of delay**, reflecting what is lost if release is delayed, but also what is gained by releasing early.

Balancing value and duration

A more objective model is the **weighted shortest job first** (**WSJF**) formula, which divides the cost of delay by the duration.

$$WSJF = \frac{Business\ Value + Time\ Criticality + Operational\ Value}{Duration}$$

Based on this relative calculation, work of similar value would be prioritized based on what can be delivered faster, while work of similar duration would be prioritized by what delivers more value.

This model implicitly encourages teams to break their work down and to discard functionality with little value.

Value flow rate

Calculating these factors can be time-consuming and unlikely to yield sufficient benefit for the additional effort. Instead, consider approximating these factors using the more abstract points – as described for sizing (see page 62).

The *value flow rate* is calculated by dividing the value by the size, and is a simpler way to objectively prioritize.

When calculated like this, it is called the **value flow rate**. Overall, this approach shifts the conversation to focusing on throughput of value rather than on economic estimates and prioritization.

Estimating and sizing

Experience of working on product development has shown that human beings are inherently flawed when it comes to estimating time or cost, especially when developing novel products.

The only time we know how long something will take is when it has been completed. There is little point in investing too much time up-front to calculate detailed estimates that will be wrong.

Comparing rather than estimating

Humans are, however, very good at comparison. We evolved the ability to assess quickly whether animals were faster than us and if they could be a threat or a meal. As a modern example, we are able to assess comparative speed, so we know when it is safe to cross the road, even though we cannot determine precise speed.

> "It is better to be roughly right, than precisely wrong."
> John Maynard Keynes (economist)

When it comes to estimating our work, we work with abstractions – most commonly, **story points** and **T-shirt sizes**.

Story points

Smaller backlog items, like stories, are typically sized with story points. This is based on the **Fibonacci sequence**, in which each number is the sum of the two preceding numbers – 1, 2, 3, 5, 8, 13, 21, 34, etc. The increasing gaps help to avoid arguing over one point more or less. In adopting this for story points, however, the sequence has been rounded off:

1, 2, 3, 5, 8, 13, then 20, 40, and 100.

T-shirt sizes

Larger bodies of work, like epics, are often sized with the more abstract T-shirt sizes, using abbreviations: S, M, L, XL, 2XL, etc.

Size is dependent on team

When a team assess the size of a backlog item, they are doing so based on the experience of working together, their familiarity with the technology involved, and their understanding of what is required. As each team is made up of different people, the same piece of work will often be sized differently between teams. This is okay, as size rarely needs to be compared across teams.

Sizing backlog items is not the same as estimating effort – size includes complexity and risk as well as effort.

Avoid the temptation of associating size with duration. Using that to create a detailed project plan will ultimately fail.

How size relates to time

Size should not be used as a measure of time, as it encompasses the three complementary concerns of **complexity**, **risk**, and **effort**.

By acknowledging that we cannot know everything before work starts, and using an abstract measure to size the work, we accept and absorb the variability that arises. For example, a three-point story might take two days on average to complete. However, this does not mean you can forecast that all three-point stories will take two days. The actual time to complete a story will be distributed along a curve. This can even mean that, at times, some lower point-sized work will take longer than some higher point-sized work. While rare, this is perfectly normal.

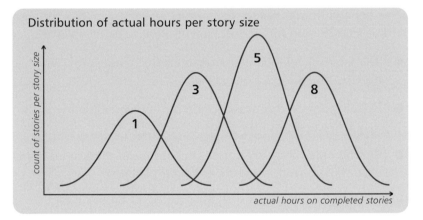

Distribution of actual hours per story size

count of stories per story size

5

3

8

1

actual hours on completed stories

Organizations should unobtrusively keep metrics on time to complete each sized story to identify trends over time. If the average increases, the team might need coaching or training. If it decreases, on the other hand, this might mean the team are improving enough to consider recalibrating how they size. High-performing teams that are reliably breaking backlog items down into similar-sized work may even be able to dispense with sizing altogether.

Just as with story points, while T-shirt sizes are not time-based, you do need to make sense of roughly determining how long a larger body of work would take. For this reason, you can create an exchange rate from abstract sizes to sprints. For example, a small T-shirt size might be thought of as roughly equivalent to a half-sprint, a medium size to a full sprint, a large size to three sprints, and an extra-large size to five sprints or more.

Continually refining the backlog

The product owner needs to ensure that sufficient items on the product backlog meet the team's definition of ready. This is done in a regular session called **backlog refinement**, which can be considered an extension of discovery workshops – except it typically involves the whole team.

Refining in advance of iteration planning

Backlog refinement happens during delivery iterations, looking at work the team might do in a future iteration, rather than further reworking the work they've already committed to in the iteration.

The number of iterations to prepare ahead depends on several factors, including dependencies, the number of teams involved, and how complicated the technical environment is. Teams should allow enough time to reduce complexity and mitigate risk through further analysis, and for any dependent work to be completed.

- The recommendation is that teams refine their product backlog for two iterations ahead.

- Refining any further ahead could mean detailing work that may become deprioritized.

- On the other hand, refining less could mean the team do not have enough work ready for iteration planning.

Some members of the team will be involved in higher-level discovery activities, but it is vital that the whole team have time to refine at a more detailed level. High-performing teams achieve this through scheduling an hour or so at the same time every week with their product owner and any specialist roles required.

Refining for success

Ensuring that the product backlog is ready will make iteration planning more effective and efficient, because the team can start planning with a clear, prioritized, and well-defined set of backlog items. It also helps the team stay clear about potential upcoming work, as the product owner might have changed priorities since their release planning session.

Breaking down, defining, and agreeing on what work might be required for the desired functionality also helps the product owner to make choices about what could be deprioritized or removed altogether.

Backlog refinement should not be used for additional analysis on work committed in the current iteration plan.

Teams that do not refine continually will lose most of their iteration planning to resolving intent and technical options.

Breaking work down to meet the INVEST criteria

When teams are successful in ensuring that their product backlog covers all the capabilities a product will require, it often ends up lumpy, with stories that vary too much in size. Stories are often too large because they are complex or have too many unknowns.

The INVEST principles (see page 56) tell us that stories should be small enough to be completed within a single iteration. By not making them small enough, the team risk not completing the work. The following techniques should help break stories down:

1 **Workflow**: Larger backlog items like epics typically cover an entire workflow – look for subsets of steps that would each still achieve an outcome of value.

2 **Complexity**: If a larger backlog item does not describe a workflow, consider whether there are hidden complexities like tricky business rules or multiple languages.

3 **Deferral**: Consider whether any part of the backlog item could be split off and deferred to a later iteration – while each backlog item should have value, that can come from feedback given on a simpler service launched first.

4 **Prioritization**: Consider whether any part of the backlog item could be split out and delivered sooner – an element that is time-critical or that other teams are dependent on.

5 **Analysis spikes**: Sometimes when a team have sized a backlog item as too large, it's because there is too much uncertainty – consider investing some time in the next iteration to do more detailed analysis or a proof of concept to get greater understanding, then use that insight in the next backlog refinement session.

The team should work through these options and document any new backlog items identified. They should also apply the same criteria for a well-formed backlog and the definition of ready.

Don't worry if occasionally the team end up with a story that is not truly independent – that is a guideline rather than a law.

Breaking backlog items down is also known as *story splitting*.

65

Transparency in discovery

As discussed earlier (see Chapter 2), transparency is a critical factor for projects to be successful. While the focus of transparency is often on **delivery** and **learning** (Chapters 5 and 6), it is also important that the organization and the project team can see – and as far as possible be part of – decision-making during discovery.

There are three key concerns for transparency in discovery:

- Understanding the discovery process itself (i.e. this chapter).

- Visibility of decisions made (see below).

- Seeing progress of all potential ideas (see opposite).

Discovery decisions

Throughout discovery, decisions are made on which potential ideas are desirable, feasible, viable, and get selected to work on.

These decisions might be strategic or tactical in nature. Strategic decisions help establish direction and alignment, and build a longer-term roadmap, while tactical decisions are typically more short-term, like what to work on in the next iteration.

Unless the whole project team are involved in these decisions, it is vital they can see what is being considered and what might be taken forward. There will also be many stakeholders outside of the team with a keen interest in how discovery is progressing.

Discovery reviews

The simplest way to make discovery decisions transparent is to display potential ideas on a discovery board (see opposite) in a column reflecting decisions made. To be fully inclusive, you might also include columns for **On hold** and **Rejected**.

Another approach, growing in popularity, is to conduct a regular review of what's happening in discovery with the whole project team and all interested stakeholders.

Just as in delivery, holding reviews for discovery has two objectives:

- Shows everyone which potential ideas have been identified and which decisions have been made or are being considered.

- Elicits feedback and facilitates open discussion, which can help uncover unexpected risks and dependencies or even other potential ideas that could be better or be combined.

Discovery board

As the team are working during each iteration, they need to see and contribute to what might be coming up next. Then, during backlog refinement, they will also want to see other potential work so that they can identify any risks and dependencies.

Just as the project team will display their delivery work in progress on a board, many teams also like to see the progress of discovery work alongside on a separate discovery board.

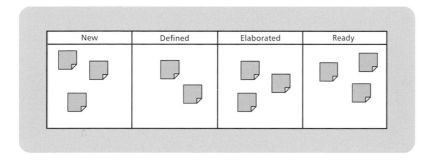

As the discovery board helps visualize the discovery process, the columns will reflect the steps specific to each organization. However, they will typically be used to depict potential ideas that are new, defined, elaborated, and ready.

- **New**: During discovery workshops, the discovery team will consider whether recent feedback and insights should result in changes to the scope, and then select the next most important deliverable(s) to be refined.

- **Defined**: Each deliverable will typically result in one or more epics that need to be named and given a brief description – at this point, dependencies should start to be identified.

- **Elaborated**: Each epic will be broken down into stories as the likely iteration to start work on it gets close – at this point, the whole project team will collaborate to agree acceptance criteria, assess any risks to be mitigated, then identify any dependent work and confirm when it should be completed.

- **Ready**: Finally, when all dependent work has been done – including graphics, legal, web copy, etc. – the stories will be refined to the team's definition of ready so that they can be considered in the next iteration planning session.

Summary

- Consider starting discovery early with a small discovery team – product owner, business analyst, and representatives of stakeholders and others who can contribute.

- The definition of ready is a shared understanding with the team, regarding how much work is required on a backlog item before the team will accept it at sprint planning.

- The product backlog is a prioritized requirements list for all the work the team need to do to complete the project.

- Work is defined at different levels of detail – epics describe large units of work like end-to-end workflows, while stories are the building blocks completed at each iteration.

- The user-story format is a common template for describing the work to be done, as well as defining who it will help and what value it will bring to them.

- To be well formed, a backlog item should meet the principles of INVEST – being independent, negotiable, valuable, estimatable, small enough, and testable.

- Acceptance criteria define how the team will know their work is acceptable – capturing what they should and should not do.

- The backlog needs to be prioritized – options include MoSCoW, forced ranking, shortest duration, highest value, weighted shortest job first (WSJF), and value flow rate.

- Rather than estimating work in hours, teams should use an abstract size that takes into account complexity and risk as well as effort – options include story points and T-shirt size.

- Backlog refinement is an ongoing activity where the team work with the product owner to progressively work on backlog items until they meet the definition of ready.

- When a backlog item is too large to be completed in a single iteration, it should be broken down – options include workflow, complexity, deferral, or prioritizing.

- Transparency is critical at all stages, and during discovery the team should ensure that their progress in preparing the backlog is visible to all interested parties.

5 Delivering for impact

Development and deployment

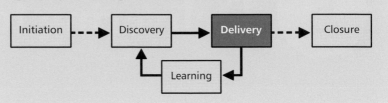

Agile project management life-cycle

Initiation ---> Discovery ---> **Delivery** ---> Closure

Discovery ---> Learning ---> Delivery

Having established good foundations during the **initiation** stage, completed some high-level **discovery**, and refined it ready to start, the work of **delivery** can begin. In place of a traditional project *work breakdown structure*, agile projects have progressive layers of planning (as we first saw in Chapter 3).

Don't forget

This model works for all frameworks, although the names will vary. With the Agile Project Framework (see Chapter 8) the iteration is a *timebox* while in Scrum (see Chapter 13) it is a *sprint*.

Planning level	Typical timeline	Level of work items completed
Project	12 months	Project milestones
Release	3 months	Large backlog items (e.g. epics)
Iteration	2 weeks	Small backlog items (e.g. stories)
Day	24 hours	Individual tasks

- The project is successful by delivering on its milestones, through completing a number of releases.

- The milestones mark when the required capabilities – defined by larger backlog items (e.g. epics) – should be operationalized.

- Those epics are broken down into a number of smaller backlog items (e.g. stories), which are delivered at each iteration.

- In turn, stories are delivered by completing the tasks that team members identified when they committed to the work.

In general terms, discovery activities (see Chapter 4) are happening at the same time as the delivery activities described in this chapter. However, at the beginning of a project, some iterations may be dedicated to just discovery before delivery starts.

For example, **Vanguard Power** committed to two iterations of discovery and developing a proof of concept, to be followed by four iterations of ongoing discovery and delivery of the solution itself.

Delivery

When the team are ready to begin delivery, they will start from the discovery work and any proofs of concept, then evolve the solution incrementally over a number of iterations.

This will continue until either the agreed number of iterations have been completed or the agreed scope has been delivered. Once that point is reached, whatever has been delivered should have been operationalized so that the organization is reaping the benefits.

Objectives

In delivery, there are three main objectives to guide the team:

- Evolve and adapt the solution incrementally toward the scope unfolding through continual discovery.

- Complete everything required to operate or support the solution once operationalized.

- Verify the solution meets acceptance criteria as well as all non-functional requirements – definition of done (see page 81).

Format of an iteration

Agile frameworks succeed by working to shorter timeframes. Depending on the delivery framework used (see Chapter 13), the delivery team will typically commit to working in one of two ways:

- **Iteration planning** (see page 72): Teams plan the whole iteration, committing to what is deliverable in that time.

- **Replenishing and pulling** (see page 74): Teams regularly top up and triage their queue, committing to work as they have capacity.

Then, broadly speaking, all iterations combine the following:

- **Daily stand-up**: Check progress and replan if needed.

- **Development**: All the design, development, testing, documentation, and other tasks required to complete the work.

- **Operationalization**: The deployment, communication, training, marketing, operational hand-over, and other change management work required to bring the evolving solution into operation and start delivering benefits.

- **Iteration review and team retrospective**: Covered in Chapter 6.

Agile projects typically fix the team size and number of iterations, then flex the scope. When scope is fixed, however, you have to be ready to invest in additional iterations.

While Kanban teams (see pages 186-187) do not formally plan their iterations, they should still do daily stand-ups, reviews, and retrospectives.

In Scrum (see Chapter 13), the iteration plan is known as the *sprint backlog*.

Iteration planning

Working collaboratively with the product owner (or equivalent), the team agree on which backlog items they can complete within a single iteration. They then determine the tasks required to successfully deliver those backlog items. This committed list of backlog items and tasks becomes the **iteration plan**.

For effective iteration planning, the team need sufficient backlog items, prioritized by the product owner and meeting the team's **definition of ready** (see page 53).

Participants
Iteration planning is a collaborative effort between the product owner (who clarifies the backlog items and their acceptance criteria), the delivery team (that define the work and effort required to complete the agreed backlog items), and the project manager, scrum master, or coach (who facilitates the event).

Timing
Iteration planning should be the first activity in each iteration. The team will need to allow enough time to select backlog items and plan the corresponding tasks. Allow up to four hours for a two-week iteration – pro rata for different-length iterations.

Agreeing on an iteration goal
To guide the product owner and team in selecting backlog items, it helps if they first agree on a goal for the iteration. This orients them toward whatever is most critical to complete in the iteration.

When there is a significant mix of work, teams will often wait until they have determined what they can commit to, then find a significant theme in that work to act as the iteration goal.

Determining capacity based on velocity
Teams that have completed several iterations already will be able to forecast what they can deliver, based on their track record. This forecast is known as **velocity** and is calculated as the sum of story points for work completed, averaged over the last few iterations.

Where the team know key people will be out for some of the iteration, they then proportionally reduce their target capacity.

For example, the **Vanguard Power** team have eight members, so if two of them will be out for the whole iteration, their velocity should be reduced by 25%.

Selecting backlog items for the iteration plan

The product owner should select backlog items they want the team to consider, and have them in the priority order they feel reflects the importance and potential value (see pages 60-61).

For each backlog item being considered:

 1 The product owner should describe the expected outcome.

2 The team ask questions to refresh their understanding so that they have confidence they can plan the tasks required.

3 If it does not meet their definition of ready, the product owner may ask them to reserve capacity in the next iteration to complete an analysis spike as part of discovery.

4 If it is ready, the team reconfirm the complexity, risk, and effort involved – sizing it in story points.

5 If the size exceeds their remaining capacity, they break it into smaller items, putting some in the backlog.

6 If they do have capacity to complete it, they add it to the iteration plan – otherwise, it either stays in the backlog for further refining or the product owner may discard it.

Repeat these steps until the running tally of story points exceeds the iteration target capacity by a small margin. Going too far over the target may not be sustainable and lead to team burn-out.

However, it is common practice to have more ready items in the backlog; that way, if the team have completed all their committed work, they could consider pulling in additional **stretch** items.

When you have no historical velocity

As new teams have no iterations on which to base their velocity, they can instead choose an arbitrary number as a target.

For example, in their first iteration, the team at **Vanguard Power** agreed on an arbitrary target of 40. From this, they planned five backlog items – four at five story points each and one at 20.

When new items are broken out during iteration planning, consider only the highest-priority ones for that iteration.

To keep the pace sustainable, teams should avoid over-committing repeatedly.

Replenishing throughout the iteration enables the team to respond sooner to changing requirements.

Although replenishment can take place once per iteration, it is usually daily or weekly.

Replenishing and pulling

The approach outlined on the previous pages showed a team committing to deliver a batch of specific work items that formed their iteration plan. An alternative approach is to use a pull-based approach, where team members only commit to work items during the iteration as they have the capacity.

For this to work, the team must have sufficient items ready to pull in. **Replenishment** is the process of topping up the team's input queue with new backlog items. While the input queue is roughly equivalent to an iteration plan, it is typically replenished several times during an iteration rather than just once at the start.

Participants

To be successful, replenishment has to be a collaboration between the delivery team, the product owner, and any stakeholders who can help the team better understand what's needed.

Meeting frequency

The frequency and timing of replenishment will depend on the type of work being done and how quickly the team move work through their workflow. Teams working with smaller items and shorter workflows will deplete their input queue faster too, and so need more frequent replenishment.

Teams with a primary focus on enhancements and support requests may need a daily replenishment, typically following a daily triage first thing in the morning, whereas teams working on more complex solutions may still have just one replenishment per iteration. The norm is weekly or biweekly (twice per week).

Replenishment criteria

To avoid pressure on the team to over-commit, the criteria for entry into the input queue have to be clear, such as:

- **Urgency**: Reflecting service-level agreements or cost of delay.

- **Value**: Return on investment (ROI) expected (increase in revenue, market share, customer satisfaction, etc.).

- **Priority**: Usually defined jointly with stakeholders.

Although the precise combination will depend on the type of work, most teams rely on an assessment of urgency and the priority set by the product owner.

Selecting backlog items for the input queue

Team members collaborate to agree on which work items they could commit to delivering until the next replenishment. The work items still need to meet the team's **definition of ready** (see page 53).

The team will normally consider potential work by **class of service**:

- **Expedite**: Work items with a critical priority and a very high cost of delay – requiring 100% dedication from the team, meaning other items already in progress may get held up or even dropped to make capacity.

- **Fixed date**: Work items with a high cost of failing to deliver on time – require more consideration before committing.

- **Standard**: Work items with a moderate cost of delay, but can tolerate longer lead times and don't require prioritizing – best dealt with in the order they were added to the backlog.

When the cost of delay is the same for all work items, it's best to treat everything as standard, as this simplifies replenishment.

Hot tip

Treating most work as *standard* will encourage stakeholders to limit what they add to the queue, giving them more flexibility and reserving expedite for anything that really needs it.

The work mix

In addition to these criteria and the classes of service described above, some teams find they are in such demand that they reserve capacity for work from different sources. This might be reflected in how the team are funded.

For example, the **Vanguard Power** team are mostly funded by the strategy and risk department, but the network operations team are contributing 30% of the funds, and have stipulated that they should be able to get 30% of the team's capacity to ensure the Outage Reporter app integrates well with their systems.

The discipline of pull-based work

This approach requires more rigor and discipline than working to an iteration plan. The temptation is to pull in a new work item whenever something in progress becomes blocked.

Instead, teams have to focus harder on completing work before starting something new. They do this by applying limits to how much they can have in progress at the same time. This helps reduce multitasking and context switching, and allows team members to focus on one task and complete it faster.

Replanning at the daily stand-up

Once the team have started to build the product, they continually monitor progress on their team board and iteration burn-down chart. Each day the team meet briefly to consider their progress and make sense of whether they need to replan. Depending on circumstances, this could be:

- Gathering around a physical team board.

- Gathering around a screen displaying a digital team board in their digital agile management tool.

- Facilitating a video call with a shared digital team board, for teams working from multiple sites or from home.

This daily gathering is known as the daily stand-up, and represents the lowest level in the agile planning onion (see page 48).

Rules of the daily stand-up

All team members are required to attend the daily stand-up. To encourage attendance, it should be held at the same time every day – normally first thing in the morning.

To help the team stay focused, the daily stand-up is timeboxed to just 10-15 minutes. While the team should share what's happening, this does not allow them time to get into detail – any impediments raised are noted and the team move on. Anyone with the knowledge or skills to discuss a potential solution waits until after the daily stand-up to talk about it (taking it *offline*).

To maintain focus, most teams adopt a format where each member takes turn in responding to three simple questions:

 What have I completed that contributes to our iteration goal?

 What do I plan to complete next that contributes to our iteration goal?

 Do I see any potential impediments that could block us from achieving our iteration goal?

These questions help them describe their progress on stories, defects, and tasks, focusing primarily on what is left to do.

The daily stand-up is a planning session for the team, not a status meeting to update managers on progress.

Beware

76

What I have completed
Each team member shares what they have **completed** – if anything – briefly and at a high level rather than an hour-by-hour breakdown. If the related card has not yet been moved on the team board, they should update that as they talk.

What I plan to complete next
Next, they share their plan for what they expect to complete before the next stand-up – if anything. This helps the rest of the team know when work might become ready for them.

Any impediments, real or potential
Finally, they share anything that could impede the team's work. This could range from their computer crashing, being blocked on a task, or becoming unavailable (e.g. for a doctor's appointment).

How the team respond to challenges
Looking at **Vanguard Power**'s iteration burn-down (see page 87), we can tell that they were having issues from day one. Let's observe what happened at some of their daily stand-ups.

- **Day two**: The team discussed the additional story they had accepted, and felt okay about – they had sized it at eight story points and believed they could complete it.

- **Day four**: In spite of completing the new eight-point story, the team were now left with the same estimate to complete as at the start of the iteration – three stories were blocked – other team members offered to help.

- **Day six**: The trend was improving, with half the scope completed – but some stories still blocked – the project manager agreed to escalate for additional support.

- **Day seven**: The team had accepted an urgent five-point story – with only three days left, they agreed to work longer hours.

- **Day nine**: They were happy with the additional hours they had worked, but still had 20 story points remaining – with only one day left, the team again committed to an extraordinary effort to get the work completed.

In the iteration review and team retrospective (see Chapter 6), we will find out what they achieved on the last day and what they learned.

Focus on what has been completed – only talking about work in progress if it is blocked.

Evolving the solution

The solution outline created in the initiation stage (see page 58) typically consists of a high-level systems architecture and a proof of concept. This is the starting point for the **evolving solution**, so called because it grows progressively as each increment of the working solution is added to the solution already delivered, until a complete solution is fully operationalized.

Purpose

This *evolving solution* shows the team's current understanding of what the organization wants, and provides tangible evidence of the progress that has been made. It also facilitates feedback from stakeholders on work so far.

This is created by the delivery team, with contributions from the subject-matter experts and business advisors attached to the project. The evolving solution could contain each of the following:

● Business and design models.

● Prototype (proof of concept).

● User documentation.

● Support documentation.

● Deliverable solution.

Business model

The business model is developed from the prioritized requirements list and the business area definition (if created). It continues to evolve during discovery as the requirements are assessed and solutions are designed. It is developed alongside the prioritized requirements list, which is, in turn, updated to reflect the analysis of requirements in the business model. The business model should:

● Expand on the detail of the requirements.

● Describe business processes that will be changed or introduced by the solution.

● Analyze any dependencies between the requirements.

● Identify products the delivery team will produce.

● Sequence the products based on business priority and technical feasibility.

Design model

The design model is developed from the prioritized requirements list, with the systems architecture and business model (if these have been created). The design model should cover the following:

- How the parts of the solution that impact on systems architecture should be developed.

- The basis of the technical acceptance criteria for the deliverable solution or relevant parts of it.

Prototypes

As the solution is being evolved, the delivery team will often reach a point where there may be alternative ways of dealing with specific requirements. There may also be different technical ways of meeting requirements. In these circumstances, building prototypes that illustrate the alternatives can often be the best way forward. These prototypes may be discarded or become part of the evolving solution. They should:

- Demonstrate any options on the preferred way of evolving the detail of the solution.

- Explore techniques or technical capabilities being considered.

User documentation

As the solution is evolving toward a deliverable solution, user documentation will usually be required. This will support the business users by telling them how to use the operationalized solution in the most effective way.

Support documentation

The support documentation provides the technical guidance that will be required by the people who will be supporting the ongoing use of the operationalized solution. It should be appropriate for the audience and also include guidance on problem diagnosis.

Deliverable solution

Once the evolving solution is ready for deployment, having passed all the technical and business acceptance tests, it should be baselined as fit for being operationalized. Even if it is not to be deployed and put into use immediately, it still constitutes a milestone deliverable that will be reflected in progress tracking and reporting.

Attitude to quality

Backlog items and their acceptance criteria focus mainly on the behaviors and expected outcomes of capabilities. This is balanced by also paying attention to quality-of-service concerns, like technical excellence and non-functional requirements.

Tracking quality

Just as teams track progress of backlog items on their team board and burn-down chart (see pages 86-87), this should also be balanced by tracking a few key non-functional metrics too:

- **Automated test coverage**: The proportion of the solution covered by automated tests, which helps avoid regression testing becoming a bottleneck as the solution grows in size.

- **Defect removal efficiency**: The proportion of defects detected and resolved before the solution is operationalized, against the number that escape into the wild – the higher, the better.

- **Aged defect analysis**: How long defects have been in the solution, by severity and urgency – the lower, the better.

Zero defects

A bold commitment to quality and technical excellence is often reflected in a policy of **zero defects**. This puts more emphasis on detecting and resolving bugs during an iteration, rather than allowing them to *escape an iteration* to become defects, or even *escape into the wild* to become incidents.

Any backlog item with bugs unresolved by the end of an iteration should be carried over into the following iteration – unless the product owner decides it is low-value enough to be dropped.

Technical debt

Product owners want to deliver as much value as possible, which can mean the team are driven very hard. However, the team can end up cutting corners, like dropping acceptance criteria or closing a backlog item even if the code and content have known bugs.

Whenever this happens, they are effectively putting some work off until a later date, which acts as a negative counterbalance to the value being added – hence the metaphor of **technical debt**.

Just as organizations can adopt a policy of zero defects, so too should they consider proactively paying down technical debt – through techniques like refactoring.

Don't forget

In reviewing metrics like these, it is always better to look at trends – whether the metric is steady, improving, or getting worse.

Definition of done

As teams work through their iteration plan or input queue, they need a clear way of understanding when a backlog item is **done**.

Ideally, a backlog item would only be classed as done when it is has been delivered and even operationalized already. This will vary from organization to organization, from capability to capability, and even from team to team.

Defining what done means

To avoid this being subjective, teams need a common agreement – their **definition of done**. Like the *definition of ready* that we learned about in Chapter 4, this is also a checklist of what must be completed for the team to be confident their work is fit for purpose. As such, it acts as *exit criteria* for the team's work.

Creating a definition of done

A well-formed definition of done needs to encompass:

- Everything the team brainstormed as necessary.

- Any organizational constraints: development guidelines, quality processes, regulations, or social concerns.

- The needs of those to whom they are delivering the solution – whether it will be delivered directly into business operations or handed off to another team (e.g. integration).

As well as using the definition of done during iteration planning, teams often post this up somewhere prominent near their workspace.

As this was **Vanguard Power**'s first iteration, they brainstormed what should be in their definition of done – see the example below:

> **Vanguard Outage Reporter definition of done**
>
> - *Deliverable reviewed and meets standards.*
> - *Deliverable fully integrated and ready to release.*
> - *Support and user docs complete.*
> - *Meets all acceptance criteria.*
> - *Security testing complete.*
> - *No outstanding bugs: any severity 1 or 2 resolved, anything lower added to backlog as a defect.*
> - *Team are ready to demonstrate the solution in iteration review.*
> - *Product owner has approved backlog item as done.*

When to deploy

To generate value or feedback early, the team should strive to create a deliverable solution at each and every iteration. That is, all backlog items the team complete in an iteration must be agreed as meeting the acceptance criteria and definition of done, and be fit to be operationalized or released to market.

Potentially deliverable solution

Ultimately, while it is the team's responsibility to ensure the work is ready to be operationalized, the decision of when to do this sits with the product owner. They may choose to wait for capabilities to be completed and added to the solution. For this reason, this is often referred to as a potentially deliverable solution.

The backlog items the team completed will be a combination of new capabilities, modifications to existing capabilities, and potentially refactoring (improvements to quality). In this way, the evolving solution should be increasing in value with each successive increment. The product owner will often choose to wait for a minimum amount of value to be added to their product before agreeing that it should be operationalized. This may take more than one iteration.

Operationalized solution

All work intended to be operationalized in an iteration should have everything in place by the end of the iteration. This helps:

- Reduce risk, by not leaving critical work undone until later.

- Improve transparency, giving confidence that it is really done.

- Increase throughput, by reducing work in progress (WIP).

The challenge of dependencies

With more complex solutions, however, the team may be dependent on other teams or even third-party organizations.

While the new capabilities might be ready, without the dependent work they might not be able to deliver the intended value. The product owner has to choose between waiting for dependent work to be completed, or operationalizing without those dependent capabilities.

To retire this risk early (i.e. minimize the risk), the team need to identify and manage dependencies as early as possible, preferably during early discovery (see Chapter 4).

Don't forget

The *potential* of *potentially deliverable* indicates only that the solution could be operationalized, not that its quality or fitness is uncertain.

The need for a release cycle

Planning ahead and monitoring work across multiple iterations allows the team to better think about when capabilities will need to be operationalized and need contribution from other teams.

For this reason, many organizations complete a higher level of release planning once per quarter. While some would argue this is not very agile, without this level of planning most organizations would not be able to operate due to these types of constraints.

Stabilizing

Waiting for other work to be completed is frustrating for the teams involved, especially as it typically leads to rework. To cope with this, some teams will reserve the last iteration of a quarter release for stabilizing the deliverable solution.

Stabilizing is also known as *hardening*.

This does mean the team stop developing new capabilities and focus instead on proving that completed capabilities – now integrated with work from other teams – are operating correctly.

In very complex environments with many inter-dependencies, this can lead to an extended stabilization that lasts for several iterations. This highlights significant organizational constraints and impediments. Every effort should be taken to find ways to mitigate, reduce, or avoid this altogether.

Multi-level definition of done

Resolving such complexities takes time, so in the meantime, some teams choose to cope by adopting a multi-level definition of done.

The more dependencies there are, the less likely an organization will see real benefit from running projects under an agile framework.

- **Story definition of done**: The quality-of-service and acceptance criteria checked on smaller work items.

- **Epic definition of done**: For complex capabilities, it may take a few iterations to complete the work, so some deliverables like training and documentation may wait until the larger work item is fully completed.

- **Release definition of done**: Organizations in heavily regulated markets often have an additional overhead to operationalizing their solutions, such as third-party security testing or complex hand-overs. These could be part of a release definition of done completed only at the end of the release.

Actively managing risk

Teams need to actively manage their risks, deciding whether something requires an immediate response or monitoring. The risk is recorded on a RAID card – which stands for risks, assumptions, impediments, and dependencies.

A single delivery team working on a simpler solution is likely to have relatively few risks to track. It is normally enough for them to show risks on their team board, providing any updates in their daily stand-ups and iteration reviews.

On the other hand, multiple teams working on a complex solution will likely have several risks to track, especially dependencies on the work of other teams. It is common for these teams to track their risks on a project-level risk board.

The risk board

As with the discovery board (see page 67) and the team board (see page 86), the risk board is organized into columns that reflect the states that a RAID card can move through.

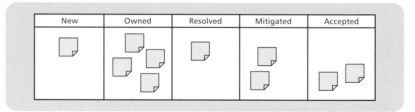

Any risk starts as new, until it is assessed and owned. The owner is then responsible for any response agreed and for monitoring the risk until it is resolved, mitigated, or accepted. This reflects the risk management process outlined in Chapter 2.

The risk radar

An alternative layout to tracking risks by state is instead to arrange them in columns according the iteration in which the impact would be felt if not resolved.

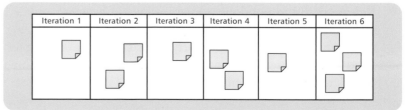

Don't forget

The risk board may also be known as a *ROAM* board, as an acronym of the states.

The radar visualization highlights the timeliness of attending to each risk, encouraging teams to focus more on those whose impact is more imminent.

At the end of each iteration, any risks or dependencies that blocked work should be converted into impediments. This should mean they are given a higher priority. Any risks or dependencies whose time has passed and that have not blocked any work are marked as either accepted or resolved.

Monitoring overall risk with a risk burn-down chart

As well as managing and tracking individual risks, teams working on complex products should consider using a risk burn-down chart to visualize overall risk throughout the release.

Whenever the team discover a risk, they assess the potential impact and likelihood to calculate a risk score (see Chapter 2).

The risk burn-down chart shows the level of overall risk on the vertical y-axis, and elapsed time (by iteration) on the horizontal x-axis.

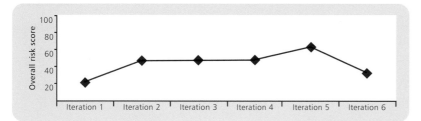

Tracking progress on the risk burn-down chart

After each iteration planning, the overall risk score is marked on the y-axis against that iteration, and joined up with a line.

As the team manage risks, assumptions, impediments, and dependencies toward being resolved, mitigated, or accepted, the risk score should reduce as the likelihood or impact is reduced. This should result in the line progressively sloping down to the right. As new risks are discovered, however, there will be an increase in overall risk, revealed by the line sloping up again.

The risk burn-down chart for the **Vanguard Power** team shows how overall risk typically increases at the start, but in this instance didn't reduce until iteration 6. When this happens, the team should explore the reasons in their next team retrospective (see Chapter 6).

Transparency in delivery

Transparency is key to success on agile projects (see page 36). This chapter covers how teams track and report progress during **delivery**, while transparency during **discovery** and **learning** is covered in Chapters 4 and 6 respectively.

Team board: monitoring task progress

Backlog item	Tasks: To do	Development	Testing	Deployment	Done

Team iteration board   *(Illustrated part way through an iteration)*

With more people working remotely, teams are increasingly relying on digital management tools rather than physical team boards.

As team members take on a task, they should move the corresponding card to the right work-in-progress column on their physical or digital team board.

If hours are being tracked, they should update any task still in progress at the end of each day with their estimate of the hours remaining.

When completed, they should move it to the *Done* column, set the hours remaining to zero, and then look for the next task for that backlog item.

When...	they should...
the next task needs another team member's skills	let the other team member know it is ready for them
the next task is dependent on another team member's task	see if the other team member needs help to complete their task
there are no more tasks under that backlog item	look for the next most important backlog item with a task they can do
there are no more new tasks or not enough time left to start one	see if any other team members need help completing their tasks

Rather than leave them all to the end of the iteration, backlog items should be reviewed and approved as *done* as soon as their last task is completed.

Once all tasks for a backlog item are completed, the card for the backlog item itself should be moved to the *Done* column. This makes it clear there are no remaining tasks for that backlog item, and that the product owner can ask for a demonstration to confirm and approve that the backlog item can be closed.

Iteration burn-down: forecasting completion

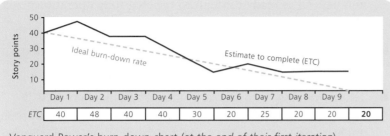

| ETC | 40 | 48 | 40 | 40 | 30 | 20 | 25 | 20 | 20 | **20** |

Vanguard Power's burn-down chart (*at the end of their first iteration*)

The **iteration burn-down chart** tracks a team's progress toward completing their iteration plan.

After iteration planning, the team plot their forecast to complete with a straight line from there to zero on the last day they could deliver something – this is their ideal burn-down rate.

The team then update the chart at the end of each day with their estimate to complete. When the team progress well, the estimate to complete would trend on or below the ideal rate. However, when the team encounter problems, the estimate to complete would appear above the ideal rate. Staying above the ideal rate for too long indicates the team are less likely to get everything done.

Teams choose whether to track a count of items remaining, the sum of story points remaining, or the sum of estimated hours remaining.

87

Release burn-up: tracking overall progress

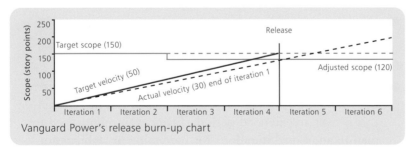

Vanguard Power's release burn-up chart

The **release burn-up chart** tracks the rate of work completed across each iteration toward the target scope. The scope is plotted after release planning, and the amount delivered added after each iteration review. This can give early warning of potential delays.

In this example, **Vanguard Power** were not delivering at the target velocity, so agreed a slightly reduced scope for the first release.

Summary

- Delivery encompasses the work from starting on a backlog item agreed as ready through to it being fully operationalized and contributing to deliver benefits.

- The team will start by agreeing the scope they will work on in the next time period.

- Teams working to timeboxed approaches, like Scrum, will conduct an iteration planning event – collaborating with their product owner to agree on a goal for the iteration, then selecting backlog items to meet that goal in their iteration plan.

- Teams working with single item flows, like Kanban, will typically replenish their input queue on a more regular basis – likely to be twice a week or even daily.

- Once per day, at the daily stand-up, the team gather for 15 minutes to review progress, consider any impediments, and replan the remaining work if needed.

- The team evolve the solution by incrementally adding to the work completed so far.

- Maintain a constant focus on quality with policies like zero-defects – never class a backlog item as done if it has any bugs.

- The definition of done establishes a shared understanding of how the team can confirm their work is acceptable.

- Work to put backlog items into operation as close to completing the development as possible – ideally as part of completing the backlog item itself.

- Where this is not possible, integrate multiple backlog items until the product owner is satisfied that it can be released – if this is over an extended period of time, you might need to plan in additional iterations for hardening or stabilization.

- Stay on top of all risks, dependencies, and assumptions – and actively manage any impediments that arise, escalating them if you cannot resolve them within the project.

- Transparency is critical at all stages, and during delivery the team should ensure their progress in delivering their work is clearly visible to all interested parties.

6 Transparency and learning

This chapter covers how the team should review their work with stakeholders and consider how well they worked as a team, to identify potential improvements.

Importance of transparency

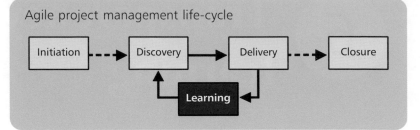

As introduced in Chapter 2, to be truly adaptive, all agile frameworks are based on the principles of empirical thinking:

- **Transparency**: Easy visibility of which activities are planned, in progress, and completed, as well as access to the solution.

- **Inspection**: Investing time to assess the work completed and the effectiveness of ways of working.

- **Adaptation**: Making the decision to improve something and then following through by doing it.

The importance of transparency

Transparency is critical to the success of organizations adopting agile ways of working, and is especially pertinent to development projects, where agile originated.

The need for transparency is often a stated value for organizations, yet it can be a difficult concept to truly grasp and implement. Without transparency there is no trust, and trust is essential for effective teamwork and for a team to be self-organizing.

A lack of transparency can be caused by things as simple as being a little discreet or ambiguous. At the opposite end of the spectrum, it can be deliberate secrecy, misrepresentation, or even a cover-up.

Typical issues seen on a team:

- Not sharing concerns about risks and dependencies until they have already become an impediment.

- Hoarding essential information or knowledge, so that people have to come to them (see forms of waste in Chapter 9).

- Misrepresenting status of work as green (i.e. good) but when you scratch the surface it is really red (known as **watermelon**).

Mindset and behavior

Transparency can be thought of as both a mindset and a behavior. People with a transparent mindset will include others by default. Teams with transparent behaviors will openly share information, whether good or bad.

Teams with a high level of transparency have:

● More alignment with each other and higher engagement.

● An increased sense of shared responsibility and accountability.

● Lower levels of risk and surprises.

However, improving transparency is not easy. Discussions can feel harder when issues are faced openly instead of trying to be polite.

How projects can be more transparent

As a leader in their organization, project managers should be a role model for transparency. Have difficult conversations earlier, to move past issues and focus on solutions. Tell it like it is; don't treat project status like a watermelon. Communicate quickly when things change. Lastly, involve others in decision-making where it makes sense and doesn't slow down progress.

It may be obvious, but still worth stating, that everyone should use visual management boards to represent the true state of work. That way, teams can see potential future work, and stakeholders can see the rate of progress. Other visual tools include: discovery boards, iteration burn-down and release burn-up charts, and risk boards (see Chapters 2, 4 and 5).

However, don't just rely on keeping charts and boards up-to-date, in the hope that people will see things. Projects should actively engage and communicate with stakeholders on a regular basis. If anything trends in the wrong direction, such as the team falling behind, make stakeholders aware of the impact promptly.

Lastly, team members must be responsible for all work items they take ownership of: updating status, progress and – in organizations using timesheets – recording their time. That way, it is easier to see when teams are interrupted by other work during an iteration (whether that work came through the product owner or was injected by a line manager), or are spending more time resolving support issues than they had allowed capacity for.

Beware

Organizations that set up long-standing teams, in value streams, are more likely to fund their teams as operational expenditure (see Chapter 11).

Engaged communication

In the preceding topic we looked at the need for transparency so that people can see the state of progress in a way that is accurate and up-to-date. For example, tracking features delivered against the full scope as forecast is a measure that should be meaningful to all project stakeholders.

Project stakeholders

Anyone with an interest in the outcomes of the project, including:

- **The business**: A term used to cover the collective interests of the whole organization's operation.

- **Customers**: Internal or external, and they include anyone who will make use of the output of the project.

- **The project team**: Both the delivery team (technical and business) and other members of the project team.

- **Suppliers**: Internal or external individuals or groups that provide anything that will be used on the project.

- **Anyone else**: Legal, financial, environmental, compliance, government, etc.

Communication plan

Once a full list of project stakeholders has been identified, we can start to put a communication plan together. This should consist of three things:

- A list of the people we need to communicate with.

- Details of what each of them needs to know.

- The method and frequency of the communication.

The project team

Communication between team members is critical to the success of the project. Poor communication is often cited as the most common cause of project failure, so it represents a key concern for effective project management.

While one of the most direct ways of communicating can be through meetings and workshops, the use of the visual management tools described on page 91 – including team boards, charts, and general whiteboards – has also been shown to be very effective.

The business

It is good practice to have some operational business roles active on the project. These can either be full-time in a delivery team or as an advisor at the project level.

Another critical role is the project sponsor, who is typically a senior leader. They need to feel confident that everything is going to plan and, if not, what is being done about it.

Effective communication

Communication is critical in an agile project, and these are the steps the project manager will need to take for it to be effective:

1 Identify all project stakeholders and their communication requirements, and document this in a communication plan.

2 It is good practice for teams to hold a daily stand-up, so ensure all team members attend and contribute.

3 Communicate progress using visual management tools such as charts, graphs, and team boards.

4 Use planning workshops to get the team fully involved in planning and taking responsibility for the plans.

5 Use velocity tracking to establish the team's capacity for work so that they can estimate more accurately based on it.

6 Make sure that all members of the team – both technical and business – are communicating effectively.

7 Keep the project sponsor in the picture by providing strategic-level communication.

8 Deliver the level of communication required by other stakeholders in line with the communication plan.

9 Review the communication plan from time to time.

Hot tip

Projects benefit from the active contribution of *subject-matter experts*, so when they cannot commit to being a full-time participant, consider an advisory role.

Iteration reviews

Assuming the team have established the **transparency** described in the last two topics, they now need to invest time in **inspection**; in this case, the latest increment of the working solution.

Preparing for the iteration review

Thinking about the iteration review should start as early as iteration planning, or even backlog refinement. The team need to consider how they will demonstrate that their work meets the acceptance criteria and the definition of done. They should design scenarios for testing that would also resonate with stakeholders.

Facilitating a successful review

While the whole team should be present, they should agree beforehand who will lead or facilitate the iteration review and who will demonstrate the solution. Facilitation follows these steps:

 1 Remind participants of the purpose for the iteration review and the time limit, and encourage constructive feedback.

 2 Explain the team's goal for that iteration, and set the scene for the demonstrations that are to follow.

 3 Compare the list of completed work items with what was committed in iteration planning, and highlight any unexpected events that had an impact on planned capacity.

4 For each item completed in that iteration:

- Explain the scenarios it was intended to cover.

- Demonstrate how it meets those scenarios.

- Elicit any concerns or ideas for additional work.

 5 Show the team's overall progress toward being ready for release (e.g. the release burn-up chart – see page 37) and capture any suggestions for what might come next.

 6 Close, by highlighting key feedback, any decisions made and actions agreed, and thank people for contributing.

Contributing to an iteration review is a good opportunity to develop public-speaking confidence as well as pride in work.

Making it worthwhile attending

Arguably, the most valuable aspect of the iteration review is getting early feedback from stakeholders, often before the solution has been operationalized. Ensure their attendance in future reviews by giving them a compelling and memorable experience.

Take the time to tell a story, by using a series of scenarios that involve real-world examples of people, places, and activities; this will make the experience far more vivid for stakeholders. If possible, have stakeholders interact with the solution; they will be far more likely to pay attention and to provide valuable feedback.

Perhaps once or twice per quarter, consider a company-wide showcase. This would not only reach far more stakeholders but it would also be good promotion for the work the team are doing.

The iteration review is a great opportunity to gather feedback and to engage with stakeholders. Do not treat it purely as a time for demo and sign-off.

Being honest about the team's progress – success and failure

In their first iteration, the team at **Vanguard Power** had three backlog items left in progress. The first had turned out to be quite complicated. The second was blocked waiting for the supplier to answer questions.

Although the work had been completed on the third item, there remained one small bug that the team had been unable to fix. The product owner suggested they class it as done, but the project manager and team felt there would be more to learn in leaving it open – the stakeholders who attended the review agreed.

Capturing feedback into the product backlog

Any significant feedback from stakeholders should be captured into the product backlog, either as additional acceptance criteria or notes for existing items, or more often as new items that build on the work just demonstrated. These new items still need to be refined and prioritized just as any others would be.

With any work the team were unable to complete, they should provide a brief explanation and indicate how much work might be left. This will guide stakeholders in their feedback:

● Treat as priority for the next iteration.

● Reassess in the next backlog refinement.

● Agree as low-value and no longer worth the effort required.

Beware

Do not wait until the end of the project before looking for lessons learned.

Don't forget

SMART actions are: Specific, Measurable, Actionable, Relevant, and Time-bound – see page 99.

Team retrospectives

After reviewing the latest increment of the working solution and getting feedback from their stakeholders, the next step of **inspection** is to reflect on how well the team have been working.

As a feedback-driven framework for leading projects, this is built on teams that make time to inspect and adapt. Before they start to prepare for their next iteration, the team should take a moment to reflect on how effective they have been.

Why we hold a retrospective every iteration

Traditionally, the project manager would wait until the end of the project to hold a *post-implementation review* (or *post-mortem*), looking back to see what lessons may be learned. While any insights may be useful, they are too late for that project, and by then people have often forgotten many of the challenges.

On agile projects, the team should hold a retrospective at the end of each and every iteration. Memories are still fresh, and changes can be made in the very next iteration. Facilitated well, this should also help foster a sense of joint ownership and self-organization.

- **Improving morale**: Teams should consider how they worked together, to highlight and deal with any misaligned behavior.

- **Improving effectiveness**: Teams should explore how effective they were, to identify any activities that could be done better.

- **Action-oriented**: Teams should agree SMART actions (see the Don't forget tip) and add them to their backlog to avoid the same challenges again.

- **High performance**: Every team should look for opportunities to continually improve toward high performance.

- **Organizational change**: Teams should escalate any serious impediments they have not been able to resolve themselves so that they can seek additional support needed to resolve whatever has been blocking them.

The team at Vanguard Power

As we have followed the team at **Vanguard Power** through their first iteration, we saw them experience a number of impediments. They were transparent about these with their stakeholders in the iteration review, and then prepared to think about the root causes in their team retrospective.

Preparing for the retrospective

The retrospective is for the team to discuss the iteration that just ended, celebrate what went well, and agree on what could be done better. While the iteration review looked at what the team built, the team retrospective looks at how they went about building it.

This should be scheduled as the final activity of the iteration, allowing up to 90 minutes for a two-week iteration.

Retrospectives need a safe space

Each delivery team has their own retrospective, so should include all team members and the product owner (or equivalent role).

It may be facilitated by the project manager, agile coach, or scrum master (if there is one), or any team member with experience.

Considering that the team may need to deal with issues relating to morale or behavior, retrospectives are normally held in a closed room to ensure privacy.

Facilitating a retrospective

The person facilitating the retrospective should follow these steps:

 Set the stage, remind everyone what the retrospective is for, and check how ready everyone is to contribute.

 Build the team's energy levels and sense of safety.

 Explore what happened in the iteration to identify successes, problems, and opportunities.

 Look for patterns and see what insights the team has.

 Analyze the main points together to agree on root causes.

 Agree on any improvement actions, add them to the backlog, and identify anything that needs to be escalated.

Teams typically use structured activities (often described as games) that shift them out of their normal thinking patterns and prepare them to contribute more openly.

Hot tip

Teams should hold their retrospective on the same day as the iteration review, as this helps them mentally end one iteration before focusing on the next.

Agreeing on improvement actions

Building on the foundations of **transparency**, and the investment the team have made in **inspection** through their iteration reviews and team retrospectives, it's now important that teams follow up with **adaptation**, improvement, and change actions.

As these reviews and retrospectives are effectively another form of discovery, teams can sometimes feel overwhelmed with options. Two effective techniques for narrowing these down and converging on actions are affinity grouping and dot-voting.

Sense-making by affinity grouping

Affinity grouping is an effective technique for identifying general themes quickly, which are then easier to prioritize and work with.

- Have all options on a whiteboard.

- Participants take turns moving an option next to another dealing with a similar concern, which will build clusters.

- If there are too many clusters, repeat the exercise to identify and combine overlapping clusters.

- Identify the theme each cluster represents, and give it a name or short phrase that describes this.

Decision-making by dot-voting

Once the team have a reasonable number of themes identified, they then need to select the most important.

Dot-voting is an effective technique for quickly agreeing on a priority, in which team members choose how to distribute a limited number of dots among the identified themes. Some teams play this game with tokens or toy money, to reinforce that team members are choosing which themes they want to invest in.

- Decide how many dots people have – typically just three.

- Participants place their dots next to whichever themes seem important to them – choosing whether to place all dots on a single one or to spread between more than one theme.

- Once all dots have been placed, count the number of dots to identify which theme has the most dots.

If several themes end up with the same number of dots, give everyone one more dot and repeat the exercise.

Don't forget

Whiteboards can be digital as well as physical.

Taking action to adapt

Having identified the most important theme to tackle, the team should now work together to agree what changes they might be able to make, or whether they have to escalate for support.

For simpler problems, the solution will be clear once the problem has been identified. For more complex problems, the team might need to brainstorm alternative ideas. If there are many possible ideas, the team should use the affinity grouping and dot-voting techniques to converge on an agreed solution.

Keeping actions SMART
It is good practice for improvement actions to be SMART:

- **Specific**: Everyone on the team understands what is required.

- **Measurable**: It is clear what a successful outcome looks like.

- **Actionable**: The team are able to implement it.

- **Relevant**: It is clear how the outcome resolves the root causes.

- **Timeboxed**: An agreed cap on how long the team should spend on it – definitely less than a single iteration.

Making team improvements visible
Once the team have agreed to an improvement action, they should ensure it is visible. Ideally, it should be added to their backlog so that it can be viewed, refined, sized, and prioritized alongside other work. This is a much more transparent way of the team negotiating with their product owner to give up some of their capacity for the next iteration to make the improvement.

However, some organizations prefer to reserve backlogs solely for work that will affect the product or service on which the team are working. In such cases, the team should find some other way to visualize their improvement action, and reduce their capacity accordingly for their next iteration planning.

From their first team retrospective, the team at **Vanguard Power** agreed three changes:

- Not to accept stories larger than 13 points at iteration planning.

- Not to accept any new stories after the iteration has started.

- Work with the discovery team to refine further ahead.

Summary

- All agile frameworks are based on the principles of empirical thinking: transparency, inspection, and adaptation.

- Transparency means making visible the activities that are planned, in progress, and completed.

- Effective communication is vital to any project, both in terms of engaged stakeholders and a healthy team environment.

- Inspection means investing time to assess the work completed and the effectiveness of ways of working.

- The iteration ends with an iteration review – the team and the stakeholders review the work just completed, assess overall progress, and update the backlog with any feedback provided.

- To generate good feedback, make it compelling and worth attending for stakeholders – rather than just another meeting.

- Be totally honest with stakeholders – celebrate the learning from what didn't go well as well as the obvious wins.

- After the iteration review, teams will normally choose to conduct their team retrospective in private so that they can safely explore what is going well with their ways of working and what might need to be improved.

- For any teams that do not have a full-time coach or facilitator, it can really help to have someone independent of the team volunteer to facilitate their retrospective.

- Teams following flow-based frameworks like Kanban may not have structured their work into iterations – however, it is still good practice to schedule reviews with stakeholders and take time out as a team to reflect on how to be better.

- Adaptation means making the decision to improve something and then following through by doing it.

- The team should add improvement actions to their product backlog and negotiate the priority with the product owner.

- In organizations where this is not possible, the team should instead reduce their planned capacity for new work so that they can invest in making the improvements they agreed on.

7 Project closure

This short chapter covers activities to close the project and what happens immediately post-project.

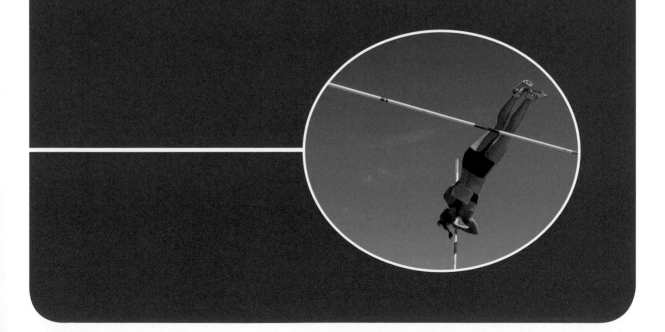

Project closure

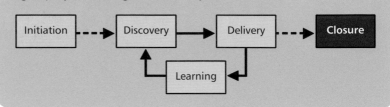

Agile project management life-cycle

Initiation → Discovery → Delivery → Closure

Learning

Once the final iteration has been completed and the solution delivered and operationalized, the project can move on to the formal stage of closure.

The project closure stage has to take care of:

Project deliverables
All the deliverables from the project should have been completed and put into operation. Formal confirmation that they have been produced to the required quality, and have been accepted by the business, should all be documented. But it is not unusual to find that some minor project deliverables have been left incomplete. Checking and confirming all deliverables will ensure they have all been completed and signed off as appropriate.

Support arrangements
The required support arrangements for the business should all have been identified as part of the requirements. These support and maintenance arrangements should now have been set up to operate for the life of the solution. The arrangements should be to operate fully within the business, unless ongoing support from the project team has already been agreed.

Lessons learned
There will normally be a lot of lessons learned (good and bad) during the course of a project. From the business point of view, it is essential that these lessons are not lost. While the project manager might well remember and benefit from these in future, it is also important that the whole business does too. Therefore, any lessons learned during the project should have been recorded, consolidated, and passed on to the appropriate group within the business for onward communication. This also forms a good basis for an organization's developing maturity in project management.

Don't forget

Try to document lessons learned throughout the project, through the retrospective, to avoid having to remember them all at the end.

102

Benefits assessment

Work to enable the benefits will have been completed during the project so that the organization starts to accrue benefits as soon as the solution has been operationalized. The solution design should also have defined how metrics would be collected to evidence those benefits – ideally as ongoing key performance indicators.

As it normally takes some time for sufficient benefits to accrue, the benefits realization review should be scheduled for an appropriate future date. It is critical that this actually takes place.

Closing the cost center

Any budget authorizations or cost centers set up for the project should be closed (or frozen) so that no further costs can be charged to the project. This means the final cost of the project, as reported in the project review, will not change.

Early project closure

If, for whatever reason, the project is terminated before completion, it should still be formally closed. In addition, the reasons for the early closure should be documented, along with any agreement on how remaining work should be handled.

Closure deliverables

Most of the project deliverables should have been produced by the end of the last iteration. However, some will be produced as part of the project closure. These include the release review, benefits enablement summary, and project retrospective.

Closure tasks

Typical tasks that will need to be carried out to close the project down include:

- Completion, sign-off and archiving of all documentation and files, and hand-over of project accommodation.

- Business acceptance should have been obtained for the solution and it should be formally operationalized.

- Technical acceptance for ongoing support should have been obtained and all technical material handed over.

- Benefits measurement should have started and the benefits realization review should have been planned.

Many project teams are disbanded before the benefits realization review can take place, so ensure someone has responsibility for this.

Schedule a thank-you celebration as part of the final retrospective.

Project success

Success in agile project management is governed by how well we pull the right levers on time, budget, scope, cost, quality, and risk. Here are the top 21 tips for success in an agile project:

 In most agile projects, cost and time are fixed and the scope is flexed, so focus on steady progress and encourage active and continual prioritization.

 The agile project manager is a facilitator and motivator, rather than an old-school task master, so lead with a light touch and keep the team happy.

 Plan the project from the strategic level down to the iterations, and allow the delivery team to organize themselves and plan the detailed work.

 The essence of agile projects is that requirements will change, so forget change control and welcome the evolving product backlog.

 Track and monitor progress at the strategic level using release burn-up charts and iterations, and share this information with the delivery team.

 Full business or customer involvement is crucial for the success of an agile project, not just by the sponsor and business management but also the real end users.

 Use the Pareto principle: 20% of the effort will deliver 80% of the benefits, so use this to appraise the plan for each iteration and release.

 All agile methods are good and complementary, so embrace whichever agile methods the delivery team and organization want to use.

 There are several excellent frameworks for managing agile projects. Spend some time up-front to determine which is going to serve your project's needs better.

10 When working to strict timeboxes, Scrum is the ideal delivery framework for the team.

 11 When working to fixed scope, consider Feature-Driven Development as an approach.

 12 When working on small items where the priority is likely to change on a daily basis, use the Kanban method.

 13 Whichever delivery framework the team use, look to Extreme Programming (XP) for a range of complementary techniques.

 14 Develop a communications plan for the project, including the daily stand-up, release burn-up charts, project dashboard, and management reports where appropriate.

15 Don't overly focus on perfection (gold-plating); in an agile project, fit for purpose is good enough.

16 Reinforce the commitment to deliver working tested solutions every iteration, to build confidence in the team.

17 Use facilitated workshops for effective brainstorming, information gathering, and decision-making.

18 Prioritize requirements, bug fixes, changes, and testing with the business; e.g. using the MoSCoW rules.

 19 Use models and prototypes to illustrate potential solutions as early as possible in the project.

20 Estimates should always be produced by the people who will do the work, and reinforced with past metrics.

21 Don't produce anything that doesn't add value to the project (see page 106 for some key deliverables).

There is an old saying that there are no good project managers, only lucky ones – so think agile and stay lucky!

Useful project deliverables

According to agile principles, nothing should be produced that does not add value (see page 14). The following deliverables have been proven to help project managers lead their agile projects:

Pre-project initiation

 Project vision (terms of reference): The objectives of the project and the reasons for carrying it out – while this might be considered optional, it does show clear direction.

 Business case: The justification for carrying out this project – also considered optional by some, it does indicate commitment or clarity at the portfolio level.

 Feasibility assessment: The results of the feasibility study, showing whether the project was feasible and viable from a business and technical perspective; helps ensure money is not wasted starting something that could be abandoned.

 Benefits realization plan: Explains how and when the organization can verify whether the project has delivered the outcomes and benefits promised at the outset.

Discovery

 Plans (roadmaps, iteration schedules, and iteration plans): Give the project team and stakeholders an overview of the whole project, a quarterly release, or an individual iteration.

 Product backlog (prioritized requirements list): A list of capabilities and work items that the project will deliver, with an indication of how critical they are to the business.

 Test plans: How the team plan to verify the product as fit for purpose before starting development.

 Change management plan: How the project team plan to operationalize the solution – including activities like training, communications, and roll-out.

Delivery

 Deployment plan: How the solution will be deployed and what other changes will be needed to ensure it can be operated successfully.

 Models and prototypes: Typically, throwaway examples of what the proposed solution could do, intended to help stakeholders get an early view or assess alternatives; the sooner people see the solution, the sooner they can provide feedback on whether it is going in the right direction.

 Burn-down/up charts: Visual indicator of progress against the iteration or release scope.

Iteration review: Every iteration should end with a review to formalize acceptance of the solution by the business, make decisions about what to do with any incomplete work, and capture any lessons to be learned for the future.

Delivered solution: The most important deliverable of all and the reason for the project; regularly releasing increments of the solution gives tangible evidence of progress, and the final delivery of the solution marks completion of the project.

Post-project

Project review and retrospective: Assesses the success of the project against the plan: Were the increments delivered on time and to budget? What was delivered, and what was not? Can the benefits now be assessed? This is what the project manager will finally be judged on.

Benefits assessment: To provide an answer to the ultimate question of whether it was worth it, comparing the final outcomes of the project with those promised at the outset, and assessing what benefits the project actually delivered.

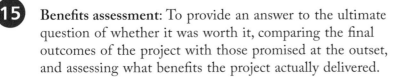
Project reviews and benefits assessments will also help to improve future projects.

Project review and retrospective

The project review and retrospective takes place after final delivery of the solution and combines the agendas of the iteration review and retrospective, looking at all deliverables and the whole elapsed period. On longer projects, this may be formalized as part of the **quarterly review and planning** event (see Chapter 10).

The project review and retrospective is also known as the *post-implementation review.*

Format

While iteration retrospectives are run separately for each team with just members of that team, the project review and retrospective should include members of all teams involved in the project, and their stakeholders.

Similar to iteration retrospectives, this would normally be run as a facilitated workshop. While the review aspect will include demonstrations and presentations, the important element is to celebrate what went well, seek feedback, and learn what could be done better.

The review and retrospective covers the following topics, and where deemed useful may also be formalized in a document:

- Release review.

- Benefits enablement.

- Final retrospective.

Release review

The release review looks at the cumulative effect of all iterations covered in the period – whether for the whole project or for the last quarter.

- Summary of what was delivered against what was forecast.

- Highlight of key decisions made and the impact they had.

- Summary of risks, impediments, and lessons learned.

Where work is to continue, the following should be included:

- Scope and priority of any remaining work.

Where this is the final iteration, it should also cover:

- Scope of any work not completed, with any recommendations for whether additional investment should be sought.

Benefits enablement review

The benefits enablement review assesses the fitness for purpose of the solution as delivered in the last increment. It links the solution to the business case by referencing each of the benefits that should now start to accrue to the business through the proper use of the solution.

- Benefits that have been fully enabled in the solution.

- Benefits that have been partially enabled in the solution, with an indication of an adjusted forecast of benefit and the impact not realizing the full benefit might have.

- Benefits that have not yet been enabled in the solution, with an explanation of why and what impact this is likely to have.

Where any benefits have not been fully enabled by the solution, the review should also cover any recommendations of what to do next, such as any workaround or to request further funds to prioritize completing that work.

Project retrospective

The project retrospective is the final component, and is dealt with last as it summarizes the impact of the whole project.

The following are suggested topics:

- A summary of the success of the project in terms of what was delivered and what was not delivered, together with any outstanding issues or actions that still need to be addressed.

- The overall cost of the project compared with the original forecasts produced during the initiation stage for the capabilities and features actually delivered.

- Records of the solution being accepted and operationalized.

- A summary of the key lessons learned regarding the project management and development processes and techniques used.

Where this is the final iteration, it should also cover:

- Confirmation of the steps to be taken to shut the project down formally, indicating what has been done already and what will be completed after the retrospective.

Hot tip

This end-project review and retrospective is likely to be what the project manager's performance will be judged on.

Benefits realization review

Organizations often neglect the benefits realization review, citing that the team are too busy or have moved on to other work. However, the underlying reasons are more likely to be that it is really hard to do, and it comes some time after project closure (when the team may have been disbanded). There may also be genuine concerns about the project's justification – which challenges governance and portfolio management processes.

Design and development of the solution should include how performance will be measured, typically through one or more metrics such as key performance indicators. It will take some time for this to be accrued; often 3, 6, or even 12 months.

Assessing the benefits

Once all the necessary metrics have been collected, the benefits review can take place. This should assess what benefits have actually accrued following the solution being operationalized.

Contents

The suggested composition of the benefits realization review report is as follows:

- **Management summary**: Overview of the assessment and success of the project.

- **Benefits accrued**: Quantitative descriptions of the actual benefits that the operationalized solution has achieved.

- **Analysis**: Highlight any differences between the actual benefits and the forecast benefits in the business case.

- **Appendices**: Details of the actual measurements, baselines, and targets used in the assessment.

Management summary

The management summary should bring together the final results of the project, reviewing the original purpose and scope, and what was delivered. It should close with an objective opinion of whether the project was a good business decision or not.

Forecast benefits

The report should itemize all of the benefits forecast in the business case, with an indication of whether they were fully enabled, partially enabled, or not enabled in the solution.

Don't forget

When benefits will be accrued in different timeframes, the benefits review should be repeated with cumulative results until a final assessment can be made.

Actual benefits

Against each of the forecast benefits, the report should show the actual benefits accrued, with the before-and-after measurement.

Analysis

Any difference between the forecast and actuals of each benefit should be highlighted, followed by an analysis of the likely causes of those differences with any appropriate actions recommended to bring future performance more in line with forecasts.

Unexpected benefits

While they should not form part of the formal assessment, it is a good idea to record any other unexpected or unforeseen benefits.

These often occur as an indirect effect of a project, and they may be difficult to quantify, as they were not forecast. These can include things such as improved cash flow, a reduced carbon footprint, or better customer satisfaction.

Appendices

Details of the actual measurements, the processes used, and any other relevant information are probably best put in an appendix to the report for any interested parties.

Quality criteria

The benefits realization review report should meet the following quality criteria:

- Does the benefits realization review cover all of the benefits expected at the start of the project and as described in the business case?

- Are the achieved benefits clearly attributable to the use of the solution delivered, or is it possible that other factors could have resulted in the figures?

- Have any variances been satisfactorily explained, as far as it is possible to do so?

Production and acceptance

The benefits realization review is often facilitated by the project manager, with input from the key stakeholders. It should be accepted by the project sponsor, who is responsible for distributing or publishing it in line with business practice.

Hot tip

The benefits assessment measures the success of the business case rather than the project – that is measured in the end-project assessment.

Summary

- Starting a project the right way is critical, but so too is closing it well – it is the last chance to make sure that everything has been completed and accepted by the business.

- There are lots of factors to being successful on a project. Keep these in mind from initiation all the way through, to ensure better outcomes.

- Other than closure activities like shutting down the cost center and ensuring all key documents are secure, the primary focus is to ensure that you conduct both a final review and a retrospective as well as a benefits realization review.

- The final review should look at the cumulative work completed and compare that to what was forecast; it should also cover the key decisions made and a high-level summary of key risks, impediments, and lessons learned.

- Also, be clear about any work not yet completed, with any recommendations for whether additional investment should be sought.

- The final retrospective reviews how the project team worked as a whole, and is different from a team retrospective, as all stakeholders would be expected to take part.

- The benefits realization plan should have determined what information will be needed, where it will come from, and who is responsible for gathering it.

- The baseline for the existing (pre-project) situation must be measured before the first release of the new solution is implemented so that the "before" figures are available.

- The benefits assessment should list all of the expected benefits together with the actual benefits achieved, with an explanation of any variances.

- There will often be additional unexpected or unidentified benefits, and it is worth recording these as well.

- While the benefits assessment measures the success of the business case, it should not be used to judge the success of the project or the project manager.

8 The Agile Project Framework

This chapter summarizes the Agile Project Framework, based on the Dynamic System Development Method, the "original" agile project management framework.

The Agile Project Framework

The **Agile Project Framework** is the most recent update to the **Dynamic Systems Development Method** (DSDM) – the "original" agile project management framework, launched in 1995. This remains the primary framework for managing agile projects. Although it was originally for software projects, it has since broadened to cover other types of business change projects.

> *The best business value emerges when projects are aligned to clear business goals, deliver frequently, and involve the collaboration of motivated and empowered people.*
> (DSDM Agile Project Framework, section 3.1)

Underlying philosophy

The Agile Project Framework is aligned well with agile values and principles (see page 14), as illustrated in its underlying philosophy:

- Address the organization, people, or process problems that cause projects to fail (see page 22).

- Nothing is built perfectly the first time, and as a rule of thumb, 80% of the solution can be produced in 20% of the time it would take to produce the complete solution.

- Things can always be completed in a later step, if necessary, because business requirements will probably change as understanding increases, so any further work could be wasted.

- Solutions developed using the method will meet the current needs of the business rather than all perceived possibilities.

- Simple solutions that are fit for purpose will be easier to maintain and modify in future.

The impact of poor communication

Managing business change and developing solutions can become more difficult when people from different disciplines or parts of an organization need to work together. Poor communication has been identified as a major cause of project failure.

The Agile Project Framework provides guidance on communication and collaboration, emphasizing human interaction, facilitated workshops, modeling, and prototyping, all of which have proven more effective than large amounts of documentation.

Don't forget

The Pareto principle, developed by Joseph Juran, states that roughly 80% of consequences come from 20% of causes.

Late delivery

Slipping timescales are a frequent occurrence on traditional projects, and preventing them is one of the key problems the Agile Project Framework deals with. Being on time is central to the model, and that applies to short-term goals as well as the project as a whole. While compromises often have to be made on a project, compromising on the deadline is not an option.

Wrong solution

Delivering a solution that does not meet the needs of the business is a frequent problem with the traditional approach to projects. Getting a true understanding of the needs of the business is central to the method. The Agile Project Framework encourages collaboration and good communication. The team are encouraged to embrace change and deal with problems as they occur, and to take on new ideas and develop a solution based on their deepening understanding of the business and its needs.

Unused features

Traditionally, businesses have tended to over-specify their requirements by wanting "every bell and whistle" that they can think of. This has led to a low percentage of the delivered features actually being used. The Agile Project Framework maintains a focus on what is important to the business, and helps it to prioritize its requirements and only develop features that will be used.

Changing requirements

Rather than regarding "changes of mind" as a problem, the method encourages them and treats changes as good things. It assumes that, with the deeper understanding that comes from developing a solution, a better solution will emerge. With iterative and incremental development and frequent reviews, the method understands and plans for change.

Delayed return on investment

Lengthy projects will often result in a delayed or even a late return on investment (ROI). By using incremental delivery, the business can start to benefit from the evolving solution as early as possible.

Gold-plating

Over-engineering, or trying to make a solution perfect, can produce an ever-diminishing return. Prioritization ensures that the business gets something good enough in a window of opportunity.

The solution needs to be fit for purpose – any more is a waste.

Principles

The Agile Project Framework is based on eight principles, intended to guide the attitude and mindset the team should adopt – as well as the design of processes, roles, responsibilities, and artifacts.

1 **Focus on the business needs**

- Understand the true business priorities.
- Establish a sound business case.
- Ensure ongoing sponsorship and commitment.
- Focus on the priorities of business-scope changes.

2 **Deliver on time**

- Constrain costs and time by working to timeboxes.
- Flex scope as required, through prioritization.
- Respect the timebox by delivering on time, every time.

3 **Collaborate**

- Involve the right stakeholders at the right time.
- Ensure team members are empowered to take decisions on behalf of those they represent.
- Recognize each stakeholder's interests (business, management, and technical), and involve them appropriately.
- Build a one-team culture.

4 **Never compromise on quality**

- Establish the required level of quality at the start.
- Ensure quality is not a variable by making verification of all work mandatory before it is classed as done.
- Adopt quality practices, like test-driven development (TDD) and testing early and continuously.
- Build quality in by constant review.

5 **Build incrementally**

- Endeavor to deliver business benefit early.
- Build on strong architectural foundations.
- Reassess priorities and feasibility after each delivery.

6 **Develop iteratively**

- Do just enough design to create a strong foundation.
- Take an iterative approach to delivery.
- Build getting feedback from customers, or their proxies, into each iteration.
- Accept that most details emerge later rather than sooner, and embrace change to get the right solution.
- Be creative, experiment, learn, and evolve.

7 **Communicate continuously**

- Run daily team stand-up sessions.
- Use facilitated workshops and encourage informal, face-to-face communication.
- Use techniques such as modeling and prototyping.
- Present the evolving solution early and often.
- Keep documentation lean and timely.
- Manage stakeholder expectations throughout.

8 **Demonstrate control**

- Measure progress through delivery of products, rather than completed activities, and make visible to all.
- Manage proactively.
- Evaluate continuing project viability based on business objectives.

Roles and responsibilities

A cornerstone of the Agile Project Framework is that the business or customer is fully involved in the development of the solution with the developer or supplier side of the project. The diagram below illustrates the project roles from the business (orange), project management (blue), and technical (green) backgrounds.

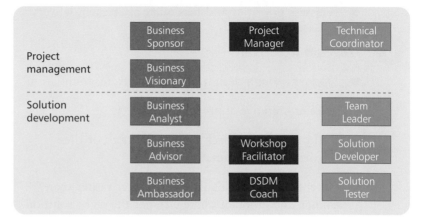

Business sponsor

This is the most senior project role. The sponsor is the champion of the project and should be an appropriate leader with sufficient authority to resolve any business issues. They are responsible for the business case, the ongoing viability of the project, and for making sure that funds, people, and other resources are made available to the project.

Project manager

Responsible for all aspects of delivering the solution to the business and coordinating all aspects of managing the project, while leaving the detailed level of planning product delivery to members of the solution development team.

Technical coordinator

The technical design authority for the project. Also responsible for ensuring the solution development team function effectively and meet the desired technical and quality standards.

Business visionary

More actively involved than the project sponsor, the business visionary is responsible for interpreting the needs of the sponsor, communicating these to the team, and ensuring they are properly represented in the business case.

Team leader

Reporting to the project manager, the team leader coordinates the work of the solution development team and ensures that products are delivered on time. In addition, they will often perform another role such as business analyst or solution developer.

Business analyst

This role is of particular relevance to IT projects, and is the link between the business and the solution developers, responsible for ensuring that the business needs are properly understood and correctly reflected in the solution developed.

Solution developer

Interprets the business requirements and produces a deployable solution that meets the functional and non-functional needs of the business. Develops models, prototypes, and deployable solutions, and documents changes to the requirements.

Solution tester

Works with the business roles to define test scenarios and test cases that will be used for testing the evolving solution. Performs tests on the developing solution and reports on the results.

Business advisor

Called upon to provide specific or specialist input to the solution developers and testers. They will often be an intended user of the solution but may also provide technical input of business rules or regulations.

Business ambassador

A representative of the business area that will use the solution. Their role is to provide information on how the solution would be used and verify that it is fit for purpose. They must be a subject-matter expert, with the responsibility and knowledge necessary to ensure that the right solution is delivered to meet the company's needs.

Workshop facilitator

Responsible for the planning, preparation, and communication of workshops but not their content.

Agile coach

Responsible for helping a team with limited experience of the method to become effective in its use.

Hot tip

On smaller projects, several roles could be fulfilled by one person.

Project life-cycle

The Agile Project Framework life-cycle is both iterative and incremental, in accordance with the principles outlined on pages 116–117. The solution will be delivered through a series of increments that build toward the final increment to complete the solution.

This project life-cycle is illustrated in the following diagram:

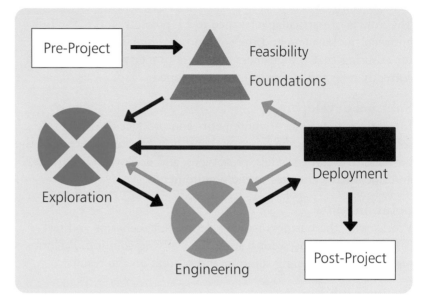

The Agile Project Framework process, as depicted in this life-cycle, consists of five stages: feasibility, foundations, exploration, engineering, and deployment. They are preceded by a pre-project phase and followed by a post-project phase.

The main path through the life-cycle is illustrated by the solid black arrows, and as it is iterative after *deployment* of each increment, the project would normally flow back to *exploration*. Alternatively, the project could return back to *engineering* if there is no new scope to explore, or even revisit *foundations* if there are significant changes or a major new release is being envisaged.

Pre-project

The pre-project stage ensures that only the right projects get started and that they are set up correctly. It describes the business problem to be addressed, identifies a project sponsor and business visionary, and confirms that the project is aligned to the business strategy. It also provides the project vision (terms of reference), and a plan and resources for the feasibility stage.

Feasibility

The feasibility stage examines the viability of the project by establishing whether there is a feasible solution to the business problem and the likely benefits that it will provide. It outlines possible approaches for delivering the solution, the type of project team that will be required, and initial estimates for the project timescale and cost.

Foundations

In a small project, the foundations stage will be combined with feasibility. Its purpose is to produce baseline high-level requirements for the project together with the business case and schedule. It outlines the proposed solution with its project management, technical, quality, risk, and life-cycle elements.

Exploration

The exploration stage will iteratively and incrementally investigate the requirements and produce models and prototypes of a viable solution for demonstration to the business. These preliminary solutions will not be fully functional or robust.

Engineering

The engineering stage turns the preliminary solution into a robust, fully-functional business solution.

Deployment

The deployment stage brings the solution into live use in the business, providing training and support for the end users where needed. It also acts as a review of the product and functionality delivered so far, with an assessment of the benefits delivered against the business case. Finally, it should decide whether the project should continue with further interim releases or should now be closed as it has delivered sufficient benefit, and the cost of further development would outweigh any further benefit.

Following the final deployment, the project will be closed and reviewed from a technical and business perspective.

Post-project

Around six months after the end of the project (or when the business benefits can actually be measured), the post-project review should examine whether the business benefits, as set out in the business case, have been met by the deployed solution.

Hot tip

This life-cycle should be configured to meet the needs of each project, with multiple *exploration* and *engineering* phases running in parallel if needed.

Don't forget

Although sometimes written as MOSCOW, the "o"s should be lowercase as they are filler vowels to ease its pronunciation as a word.

Prioritization

As the main variable on an agile project is the scope, it stands to reason that these requirements must be prioritized so that the ones that really matter to the business get dealt with. The most straightforward method of prioritization is known as **MoSCoW**.

MoSCoW rules

These rules should be agreed with the business users before the requirements gathering starts. The requirements are categorized into one of: **must** have, **should** have, **could** have and **won't** have this time. The definition of each category is as follows:

Must have

Must have requirements are the features that have to be included in the delivered solution. Failure to deliver these would mean the solution would not be usable or that the business case would not be met. They form the minimum usable subset that the project guarantees to deliver.

Should have

Should have requirements are deemed to be important to the business, although perhaps not vital. While there may be some pain if they are not included, the solution would still be viable. Their exclusion may involve the need for some form of workaround or may make the solution less efficient or effective.

Could have

Could have requirements are desirable features but less critical than *should have* requirements. Leaving them out will have less impact on the business than *should haves*.

Won't have this time

Finally, *won't have* requirements are those that the project team have agreed not to deliver in the current release. They are still documented, as they help to clarify the scope of the project and they may still make it into the solution as part of a later release.

Having agreed on a definition of these categories for prioritizing requirements, it is then up to the business to justify why any particular requirement is a *must have* or *should have*.

Following each release of the solution, all remaining unsatisfied requirements should be reprioritized, and can be promoted or demoted according to how critical they are to the next release.

Rules of thumb

As a rough rule of thumb, the *must have* scope should not exceed 60% of the project. This results in an effective contingency of 40% of the total effort of the project. Assuming the *should haves* and *could haves* are split equally, this means it is quite likely that the *should haves* can be included and still have a 20% contingency.

At the start of a project, requirements will likely be high-level and all considered as *must have*. During the project, requirements will progressively be broken down into lower-level requirements, and at this stage, other categories should start to be assigned.

Assigning priorities

As an approach to assigning priorities, first ensure the business is fully on board with the MoSCoW rules, and then:

1 Start out with all the requirements defined as *won't haves* and get the business to justify why they need them.

2 Challenge all *must haves* to ensure they really are "show stoppers" and not just nice to have.

3 Find out why each requirement is needed for the project or the next release of the solution.

4 If there is more than one requirement implied in any requirement, break it down to detail them, then check if they are the same priority or if some are not necessary.

5 Every requirement should be traceable to a project objective; if the objective is not a *must have* then the requirement should not be either.

6 Remember that priorities can change, so re-evaluate them after each release of the solution.

7 Any defects should also be prioritized using MoSCoW.

Remember that if you have many more than 60% *must haves*, it will pose a serious risk to the success of the project.

Hot tip

Challenge all *must have* requirements, and ensure they really have to be included.

Timeboxing

In the Agile Project Framework, timeboxing is a key technique for controlling the delivery of products in an iterative environment. Used with prioritized requirements it can ensure that each timebox is completed on time and every time.

Timebox control

Each timebox starts with a kick-off and ends with a close-out. In between these, the timebox passes through three steps: investigation, refinement, and consolidation.

Kick-off

Also known as **iteration planning**, this meeting starts with the team reviewing the timebox objectives and confirming that they are still achievable. They then agree on acceptance criteria for each of the products being delivered. The availability of team members to do the necessary work is confirmed, together with any external dependencies and the risks of their non-availability. Finally, the team should ensure they have a mix of priority requirements in line with the MoSCoW rules (see page 122).

Investigation

During investigation, which should typically take 10% to 20% of the timebox, the solution developers work closely with the business ambassadors investigating the requirements and how best they can be met. Where possible, an initial prototype of the solution should be created to communicate the proposed solution.

Refinement

The majority of the development work (typically 60% to 80%) will be carried out in refinement. The work will be divided up and the priorities and delivery schedule agreed. As much of the work as possible will then be completed, including testing. The refinement step then ends with a review of the work and what is needed to achieve completion. No new work should be started after this point, and any changes requested should be prioritized.

Consolidation

In the consolidation step, any actions agreed at the review are carried out, together with any further work to ensure the products meet their acceptance criteria. Quality assurance is then performed to confirm the products meet the required standard and are fit for purpose. Any products that fail in this respect are deemed not to have been delivered.

Close-out

Also known as the **iteration review**, the purpose of the close-out meeting is to record the formal acceptance by the business of the products delivered by the timebox. It also has to decide what to do about any work that was included in the timebox but was not completed. This work can be considered for a future timebox or dropped completely. Finally, the timebox should be reviewed for any lessons learned to be passed on to future timeboxes.

If practical, the close-out meeting could then run back to back with the kick-off for the next timebox.

Daily stand-up

The team working on a timebox should meet every day for a short stand-up meeting. This will normally be facilitated by the team leader and is a daily opportunity to understand how well the team are progressing toward their objectives and any issues that have been encountered. It is a short meeting of no more than 15 minutes, held in the team's workplace.

Each team member has a couple of minutes to say what they have achieved since the last stand-up, what they plan to complete by the next stand-up, and any issues (problems) or risks they have encountered. It is the way the team track progress, and provides early notice of delays and the need to replan.

Change control

As the products of the timebox are constantly being refined by the team review, it is essential that the team members and – particularly – the business ambassador have the authority to make decisions about changes. So, there is no formal change control process in place as long as any changes are within the agreed scope.

Timebox scheduling

The overall delivery plan will provide a schedule of the increments, and within each of these, the timeboxes that will make up the increments. The schedule should therefore show the number and duration of each timebox in the current increment.

Using this timebox technique with clearly prioritized requirements will ensure that each timebox is completed on time, with the highest-priority requirements. This will mean the increment will also be completed on time, and likewise the project itself.

Iterative development

Iterative development is fundamental to evolving the solution from the initial high-level requirements to a delivered solution. The Agile Project Framework recommends teams follow an iterative development cycle for each feature they work on. The cycle has four steps of: identify, plan, evolve, and review (see below):

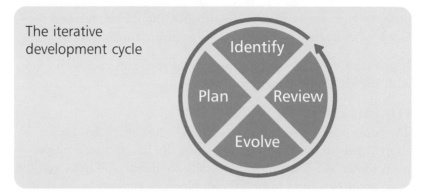

The iterative development cycle

Identify
During this part of the cycle, the delivery team agree on the objectives for whatever it is that they are developing.

Plan
The team then agree on what needs to be done and by whom, in order to meet the objectives they have defined.

Evolve
Next, the planned activities are carried out by the team in the agreed timebox.

Review
Finally, the results of the activities are reviewed to see if the objectives have been achieved. If they have been achieved then the changes are accepted, and the cycle begins again by identifying objectives for the next cycle, and so on.

If the objectives have not been met, the team will either:

- Reject the changes and go back to the previous version, or

- Identify remedial work that will be required to meet the objectives.

In either event, a new cycle will begin by identifying objectives for the next cycle.

Managing the process

Each cycle should:

- Be as short as possible, usually one or two days, with several cycles within a single timebox.

- Be as informal as possible – in most cases, an informal cycle of conversations, thought, and action.

- Involve as few people as possible – a developer and an end user may be enough for something simple, although more complex work might need the whole team and subject-matter experts.

Conversations, thought, and action

Each cycle begins and ends with a conversation, with the first conversation discussing and agreeing what needs to be done. The cycle continues with consideration of how to address what was agreed. This should take no more than 10% to 20% of the cycle.

The feature is then worked on until it meets the agreed criteria, which is typically where 60% to 80% of the work is.

The cycle concludes, once work is completed, with a further conversation to decide whether what was produced is good enough or whether another cycle might be needed. Again, this should take no more than 10% to 20% of the cycle.

Development strategy

The solution is considered to have a number of architectural layers, such as database, business rules, and user interface. In iterative development, teams may follow an approach in which each timebox delivers horizontal slices of the solution, vertical slices, or a hybrid combination of the two.

- **Horizontal approach**: The solution is worked on by architectural layers – while some teams prefer this approach, there is no working solution until all layers are complete.

- **Vertical approach**: Each feature is really a thin slice through all architectural layers – a working solution is delivered for each timebox, but the full solution may not be known until later.

- **Hybrid approach**: Where one or two architectural layers are developed first as a foundation, then everything else is vertical slices – thought to combine the best of both.

Summary

- The Agile Project Framework is an approach to developing quality business solutions in a short timeframe.

- The Agile Project Framework helps to prevent poor communication, late delivery, wrong solution, unused features, changing requirements, delayed returns, and gold-plating.

- It is based on eight principles: focus on the business need; deliver on time; collaborate; never compromise on quality; build incrementally; develop iteratively; communicate continuously; and demonstrate control.

- The project life-cycle has five stages: feasibility, foundations, exploration, engineering, and deployment. These are preceded by a pre-project stage and followed by a post-project stage.

- The framework defines 13 roles, from the business sponsor down to the workshop facilitator and agile coach.

- Facilitated workshops are a powerful tool for harnessing the strength of the team.

- The MoSCoW Rules prioritize requirements as: must have, *should have*, *could have*, and *won't have this time*.

- The iterative development cycle consists of four stages: identify (to set the objectives), plan (what is going to be done), evolve (carry out the plan), and review (the results).

- Models, prototypes, storyboards, and other techniques provide a rich method of communicating requirements and proposed solutions.

- Timeboxing is the mechanism for controlling the delivery time while allowing the number of requirements to vary.

- Estimating consists of working out how much of the requirements can be delivered in the available time.

- Quality requirements need to be defined at the start of the project and reviewed in a non-intrusive way.

- Although agile projects do reduce some traditional risks, they also introduce some risks through their dependence on the collaboration between the business and the developers.

9 Agile projects with lean principles

Lean principles are based on the elimination of waste in all its forms. This chapter explores how these principles can help in leading some types of agile projects.

Solution

Lean approach to agile projects

Lean project management evolved from lean manufacturing approaches in the automotive industry. A *lean process* is one that considers the expenditure of resources for any purpose, other than the creation of value, to be wasteful and thus to be eliminated, in order to maximize customer satisfaction and return on investment (ROI).

Philosophy

Lean manufacturing is a management philosophy best exemplified by the Toyota Production System. Toyota's growth, from a small company to one of the world's largest automobile manufacturers, has illustrated the benefits that can be achieved.

Lean has three types of waste: *muda* (inefficiency), *mura* (unevenness), and *muri* (unreasonable work; e.g. as imposed by management).

Muri focuses on what can be avoided by design. *Mura* focuses on designing a process that eliminates fluctuations. *Muda* seeks to remove inefficiencies that cause distracting fluctuations in output.

The eight inefficiencies

Originally, there were seven inefficiencies (*muda*); these were subsequently expanded to eight by adding non-use of talent.

- **Defects**: Technical debt – waste comes from having to inspect for defects and then the rework to fix any found.

- **Overproduction**: Unnecessary features – producing something before there is demand, especially if it ends up not being needed.

- **Waiting**: Idle time – waiting for information or items to arrive from another process.

- **Non-use of talent**: Not using people to the fullest of their experience, abilities, and confidence.

- **Transport**: Having to move things that are not involved in the process, before the process can be performed.

- **Inventory**: Items or information in a queue with no work being done, but unable to complete and deliver for value.

- **Motion**: Task-switching – people, material or equipment moving more than required to perform the processing.

- **Extra processing**: Doing more work than required, whether from *gold-plating* or due to poor design or poor tools.

Lean concepts for project management

Although manufacturing is a very different business domain from projects, this lean thinking can be applied to thinking about how to lead agile projects in a lean and efficient way. This can be summarized through the following 14 concepts:

● Base management decisions on a long-term philosophy – if necessary, at the expense of short-term financial goals.

● Move toward flow, and move to ever-smaller batch sizes and cycle times so as to deliver value fast and expose weaknesses.

● Use pull (demand) systems that leave commitment to as late as possible.

● Level the work to reduce variability and overburdening so as to remove unevenness in the process.

● Build a culture of stopping and fixing problems and teach everyone to study problems methodically.

● Master the practices being used so as to enable continual improvement and employee empowerment.

● Use simple visual management to reveal problems and coordinate activities.

● Use only well-tested technology that serves the people and the processes they use.

● Grow leaders from within who thoroughly understand the work, live the philosophy, and teach it to others.

● Develop exceptional people and teams that understand and follow the company's philosophy.

● Respect your extended network of partners by challenging them to grow and helping them to improve.

● Go and see for yourself at the real place of work in order to understand the situation and provide useful help.

● Make decisions slowly, by consensus, thoroughly considering all the options, then implement them rapidly.

● Become and sustain a learning organization through relentless reflection and the practice of Kaizen (see page 137).

Don't forget

Also known as *walking the floor* and *going to the Gemba.*

These five principles were first described in the book *The Machine that Changed the World*, by Womack, Jones, and Roos.

Lean principles

From its origins in manufacturing, lean thinking encourages the practice of continual improvement and has transformed the world of knowledge work, including projects. The lean concepts discussed earlier are underpinned by the following five principles:

Identify value

Focus on how stakeholders see value in a product or service, then strip away nonessential steps to deliver to that value. In a project context, this champions project outcomes as a means of prioritizing what gets done and avoids unnecessary work.

Map the value stream

In manufacturing, the value stream is the complete sequence of activities involved in building and delivering an end product. These are typically visualized with a **value stream map** (see below) or state transition charts. When applied to projects, this means identifying the steps each work item must go through.

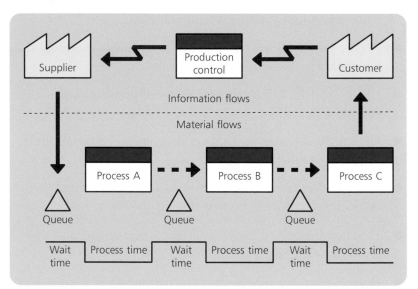

Enable value to flow

The value stream map helps to identify what is essential and to optimize the rate and evenness with which work flows. This also helps eliminate queues of excess, or early or unexpected inventory. On projects, this should lead to reworking the project approach, eliminating any steps that add little or no value, or combining steps that could be completed at the same time. This also reduces queues of work for anyone working "downstream".

Let the customer pull value

Traditionally, manufacturing was based on a push approach, where targets were set from a predetermined schedule and production quota. This approach is not responsive to customer demand, and typically led to overstocking unwanted items or not being able to supply enough of what was wanted.

On traditional plan-driven projects, the wasteful effects of this push approach would be seen in the significant time invested in collecting requirements, completing analysis, and designing the whole solution before anything got developed. This is costly when requirements change; even more so when the organization subsequently decides it would rather invest in a different project.

A pull approach in manufacturing, on the other hand, only puts something into production when there is demand for it. To deliver in a timely manner, this depends on accurate forecasts combined with a streamlined and adaptive production process. This should cut waste significantly and increase customer satisfaction.

Switching to pull over push ensures that the requirements being worked on are always fresh and high-priority.

Of all five principles, this probably presents the biggest challenge from a project perspective. Switching to pull-based flow on projects means frequently refreshing the priority of requested work, and committing to items only when there is capacity. This helps keep focus on work that is already in progress, reducing wait times, and getting to completion faster. **Kanban** is the most popular lean delivery framework (see Chapter 13).

Improve continually

The process of lean project management itself should be treated as iterative and incremental. While a waste-free process might be practically unattainable, having this as a goal should drive for constant improvement.

This is closely aligned with the agile principle of the team regularly pausing to reflect and look for opportunities to improve, and is most commonly seen as retrospectives (see page 15).

The Japanese concept of *Kaizen* (*improvement*) describes this practice, especially highlighting that it involves all team members.

Other principles

Other key principles in lean project management include how to amplify learning, decide as late as possible, deliver as fast as possible, empower the team, build in integrity, and see the whole picture. Some of these are explored on the following pages.

Lean project teams

The heart of any project is the team, which need to be provided the space and support to collaborate. It is vital that both the team and the leaders providing support understand these lean principles.

Lean project teams

While any team could be described as a group of people who depend on each other to work toward a common objective, lean teams need specific lean teamwork practices.

- Even if temporary, the project team should regard themselves as part of the value stream they are serving.

- Effective project teams reflect their value streams by being dedicated to the project, long-lived and constantly improving.

- Lean project teams transcend traditional functional silos, being fully cross-functional, with all the skills needed to deliver on their objectives.

- To improve communication, collaboration, and interaction, teams should be as integrated as possible, bringing in those roles traditionally considered to be stakeholders.

- Team building, development, and performance improvement activities are performed by the integrated team.

- Leaner project management needs self-organizing teams, with the autonomy to decide for themselves what to do and how.

- Work items are assigned by the team members themselves, deciding who does what, when and how.

Lean project leadership

With decision-making delegated, the role of leadership changes, focusing on a supportive environment and empowering the team.

- Providing the team with training, coaching, and mentoring to gain self-organizing skills.

- Creating an environment of psychological safety, free of fear, where mistakes are seen as a means of learning.

- Recognizing team performance rather than assessing individual accomplishments, which acts against teamwork.

- Selecting team members to achieve a balance and personality fit.

Lean project life-cycle

A project's life-cycle is the sequence of stages and steps from validating an idea to realizing the benefits of implementing that idea. The lean project life-cycle has the following stages:

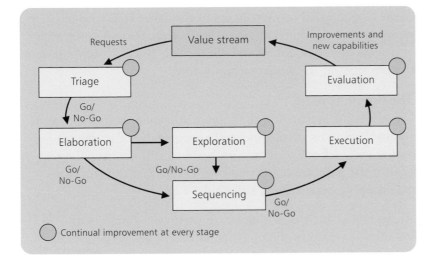

There is a go/no-go decision at every stage. Although the request could be rejected, this is a good outcome as it helps focus on higher-value requests.

- **Triage**: Rapid assessment of a request's suitability and urgency, confirming that it is aligned and desirable.

- **Elaboration**: Adding description, objectives, root cause, and solution options; the request could be queued either for *sequencing* or with more complex requests for *exploration*.

- **Exploration**: An optional stage to undertake research, analysis, feasibility, or prototyping that could help validate the request, following which the request could be queued for *sequencing*.

- **Sequencing**: Candidate requests are given a schedule priority and sequenced ready for intake replenishment into *execution*.

- **Execution**: As the team have capacity, they pull requests off the intake queue, creating deliverables and putting them into operation within the value stream.

- **Evaluation**: After completion, the team will review to see what they could do better in future, and then some time later there is a review against the project objectives.

- **Continual improvement**: At every stage, the team should pause regularly to reflect on how well they are working and what could be improved (see the blue dots in the diagram).

Seeing the whole

Great products, services, or processes are not just the sum of their parts, but are also the product of their interactions; that is, how the different components work when they are integrated. Defects can accumulate during the development process. By breaking down requirements or work items into smaller tasks and by standardizing the different stages of development, the root causes of defects should be found and eliminated. But it is still important to keep sight of the whole or big picture.

The big picture

The larger the system and the more disparate organizations that are involved in its development, the greater the importance of having well-defined relationships between different suppliers. Even if the parts are developed by different teams in the same organization, these criteria still apply.

At the end of the day, the aim is to produce a system with smoothly interacting components. During a longer period of development it is much more critical to have a strong sub-contractor network than to optimize short-term profitability. The aim is to get everyone on the project – no matter who they work for – into a win-win relationship.

Lean thinking

Lean thinking has to be well understood by all members of a project team before they begin to implement the required situation. This may indicate the need for some sort of workshop on the principles if they are not all from the same background.

> **Think big, act small, fail fast, and learn rapidly.**

This slogan sums up the lean principles for the whole project management process, and seeing the big picture is the starting point. Small increments and tasks satisfy the second part. Delivering fast ensures that failures are spotted quickly so that they can be rectified. Amplified learning ensures that everyone in the team learns quickly and effectively from each other's learnings.

Only when all the lean principles come together, combined with a good common-sense approach and with respect for the working environment, is there a basis for success in software development.

Amplifying learning

Amplifying learning

Project delivery is a continuous learning process. It requires an exploratory approach for problem-solving, and the results of this should provide insights. Teams with highly specialized skills face the additional challenge of sharing knowledge within the team. The best approach for improving a project team environment is by looking for ways to amplify or communicate the learning.

Show and tell

Requirements elicitation is a process that can be simplified by developing basic screens, demonstrating them to the users, and getting their feedback. In a similar way, different ideas can be tried by writing the code and showing the results to the users. This can be far more effective than adding more detailed design documentation or specifications. By running tests with the users as soon as the code is written, the developers can get instant feedback and prevent any further wasted effort.

Short iterations

The learning process can also be accelerated by short iteration cycles, each culminating in integration testing and customer demonstration. Improved customer feedback will help establish where the current phase of development is and what changes need to be made for future improvements. During these sessions, the customer representatives and development team will learn more about any problems and review possible solutions for further development. This way, the customer can explain their needs better and the developers can understand better how to satisfy those needs.

Set-based development

Another technique in the communication and learning process with the customer is the use of set-based development. This focuses on the constraints of the future solution and not the possible solutions. This promotes development of the solution through dialog with the customer.

Kaizen

Kaizen is Japanese for improvement. It is a practice that focuses on the continual improvement of processes. It is based on a cycle of identifying problems (or opportunities), discussing them with colleagues, proposing improvements to the process, and then implementing them. It is another way of amplifying learning.

Deciding late

Project management is always associated with some degree of uncertainty. Therefore, better results should be achieved by making decisions as late as possible in the process. This means all available options are kept open until a decision can be made based on facts and not on assumptions or predictions of outcomes.

The more complex the system, the more capacity for change should be built into it. This will enable the delay of important and crucial commitments to the last responsible moment – and make it more possible to adapt to changing requirements.

Iterative approach

The iterative and adaptive approach promotes this principle, with the ability to adapt to changes as they are discovered and correct mistakes as they are identified. These changes and mistakes could otherwise be very costly to correct if they only come to light after the system is operational.

Due to its flexible nature, this lean project management approach can actually allow some capabilities to be delivered earlier. This, in turn, can allow the delay of any crucial decisions until stakeholders have fully understood their needs and potential solutions to them.

Planning

In the lean project environment, planning activities should concentrate on the different options available based on the current situation. Once the different options have been costed in terms of time and other resources required for their implementation, the customer is likely to make a much better decision on the way forward. This, once again, provides the flexibility required for late decision-making.

Set-based design

Another idea from Toyota is set-based design. If a new capability is needed, several teams could be tasked with designing a solution to the same requirement. As each team learns more about the requirement, they design a potential solution.

If any potential solutions are deemed unsuitable by stakeholders, they are dropped. At the end of the designated period, the remaining designs are compared and the best is chosen, possibly with some modifications based on learning or combining ideas from multiple teams.

Hot tip

Keep all your options open until you have to make a decision.

Don't forget

Models and prototypes can help communicate potential solutions.

Delivering fast

Sometimes, project delivery can seem to take forever. People hit problems and take a long time thinking about and fixing them, or they make things complicated rather than keeping them simple.

In an era of rapid evolution, it is not the biggest that survives, but the one that adapts the fastest. The quicker the end product can be delivered, the sooner stakeholders can start to benefit and the sooner feedback can be received, for incorporation into the next iteration.

Short iterations

The shorter the iterations, the better the feedback, learning, and communication within the team. With a shorter duration, decisions can be delayed. Speed assures the fulfillment of the customer's present needs, and not what they required yesterday or tomorrow. This gives them the opportunity to delay making up their minds about what they really require until they gain better knowledge of the potential final product. Customers also value rapid delivery of a quality product.

Just in time

The lean production approach known as **just in time** can also apply in the world of projects. Stakeholders can present the required results to the team in a simple way using simple requirements, in the form of small work items (like **stories**), and then leave the team to organize themselves and allocate the work.

The team can then get on with estimating the time they will need for the implementation of each work item. The work organization becomes a self-pulling system. As with other agile approaches, the team meet every day for a stand-up meeting, to help focus on completing work and resolving any impediments in the way of progress.

Set-based design

Toyota's set-based design was introduced in the previous topic. This also enables fast delivery by the developers of parallel potential solutions, rather than by trying one solution at a time with the inherent delay if the first potential solution is not suitable.

To deliver fast, get the right people, keep the product simple, work as a team, eliminate waste, and build in quality.

Eliminating waste

Value has been defined as anything the customer is prepared to pay for. So, anything not adding value to the customer is considered to be waste. In a software development environment, this includes:

Unnecessary code
Unnecessary code or functionality is a waste. Partially done coding that is abandoned later in the development process is a waste. Extra processes and features not used by customers are all waste.

Delays
Any delay in the software development process is a waste. Waiting for other activities, teams or processes to be completed is a waste. Defects and lower quality cause delay and are waste. Filling out documentation or writing reports causes delay and are waste.

Unclear requirements
Poorly defined or imprecise requirements are a waste. They will either result in the wrong functions being developed or time being wasted while they are cleared up.

Inadequate testing
Insufficient or inadequate testing can lead to wasted work needing to be corrected or rewritten. Automated testing can help to eliminate this.

Bureaucracy
Management bureaucracy such as unnecessary documentation that can hinder the rapid development of code is a waste.

Poor communication
Slow internal communication that can result in wasted effort or delays to work is a waste.

In order to eliminate waste, we have to be able to recognize it. There are many techniques that can be used to examine a process and identify where value is added to the product. The same techniques can also be used to identify and recognize waste. If an activity could be skipped or the required results could still be achieved without it, then it is waste.

Having identified waste, the next step is to examine the sources and then eliminate them. This should be an iterative process until all non-essential processes and procedures have been removed.

Never stop looking for waste and then eliminating it.

Improving the flow of work in progress

Flow is commonly based on the queueing theory that the time it takes to complete a work item is a factor of the amount of work in progress and the average completion rate. This focuses attention on optimizing the rate and evenness with which work flows.

Focus on flow

- **Reduce friction in the workflow**: Design a process for work to proceed immediately to the next step without stopping.

- **Optimize for throughput, not utilization**: Make work items smaller and reduce the number in progress at the same time.

Minimize handling work items in batches

Avoid moving multiple items from one step to the next at the same time – excessive batching will create unnecessary queues, hand-off points, and delays. There are many types of batches:

- **Projects**: The project is a container for many types of work – focus on using this to coordinate between functional areas, rather than implementing them all at the same time.

- **Budgets**: Organizations use budgets to assign funds to areas of strategic importance, typically on an annual, half-yearly, or quarterly basis – recognize this as trying to guide outcomes, rather than a shopping list that has to be delivered together.

- **Releases**: Unmanaged dependencies will get in the way of smooth flow and agility – either remove them by enabling your project to do the work instead, or orchestrate around them by scheduling work to accommodate these timelines.

Pull work into progress when there is capacity

- **Limit work to capacity**: Work should be pulled in when there is capacity to do it.

- **Constrain demand to capacity**: Put caps on the work intake queue so that stakeholders know work has to be completed and will drop scope if they need something sooner.

- **Simplify prioritization to FIFO**: If queues are kept short, then the work can simply be pulled in the order it was added.

- **Level the workload**: Work to a regular cadence or timebox, rather than flexing it depending on the work – stakeholders will naturally keep their requests smaller.

This queueing theory is commonly known as *Little's Law*.

First-in first-out (FIFO) is an entry-sequenced queueing approach.

Summary

- Lean approaches to project management evolved from lean production processes developed in the automotive industry.

- The basis of lean philosophy is the elimination of waste, which is anything that does not create value for the customer.

- Applied to knowledge work, this became the five principles of: identify the value, map the value stream, enable the value to flow, switch to pulling work, and improve continually.

- Identify value by focusing on what stakeholders see as valuable and strip away anything non-essential – be ruthless if referencing project outcomes to avoid unnecessary work.

- Map the value stream by visualizing everything that touches the work from request to delivery, both in terms of what adds value and what does not.

- Enable the value to flow by eliminating any steps that add little or no value – like batching work up for different teams.

- Switching to pulling work only when there is demand downstream – focus on work in progress and get it done faster.

- Improve continually by pausing to reflect and consider what could be done better – like the iteration review.

- The replenishment step in a lean project life-cycle is based on: triaging requests as soon as possible, adding any new information, optionally taking time to analyze more complex requests, then sequencing for class of service ready for work.

- It is important to see the whole (the big picture) and to keep all parts of the development team working toward the same aim, particularly if it is a dispersed or multi-supplier team.

- Making decisions as late as possible removes uncertainty, allows options to be kept open, ensures that decisions are made based on fact, and allows a more complete understanding of the problems.

- Delivering as quickly as possible means that the customer can start to get benefit from the product sooner and provide feedback more quickly.

10 Agile in controlled environments

Heavily regulated environments are deemed to suit more plan-driven program management approaches. This chapter shows how to work within those constraints to discover, deliver, and learn in a more agile way.

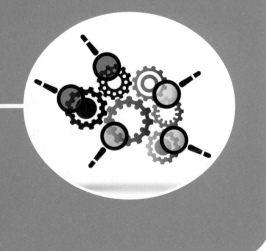

Controlled environments

Organizations that operate in regulated industries have to comply with the rules and guidelines defined by regulators. This is designed to protect the legitimate interests of businesses and communities by regulating appropriate activities and behaviors. Projects running in these organizations have to allow for the overhead of governance, risk, and compliance.

Projects in controlled environments

Project frameworks that incorporate these overheads were formalized in the 1970s by the US and UK governments for use with their suppliers. Due to the widespread use of these frameworks, these became the *de facto* approach for many organizations, even those not working with governments.

Projects in Controlled Environments (known as PRINCE) is one example from the UK. Although initially seen by many as the epitome of the *waterfall* approach, this has evolved to support agile projects too. This chapter is based on **PRINCE2 Agile**.

Controlled tolerances for project constraints

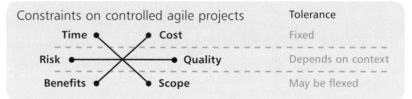

All projects should understand their constraints, agree tolerances for these, and then ensure the project keeps within them. For most projects, this is based on the triple constraints (see page 12):

- **Time**: Investment is normally for a fixed number of iterations.

- **Cost**: A stable team for the duration also fixes the costs.

- **Scope**: Other than for essential items, scope can be flexed.

Managing projects successfully in controlled environments includes three more common constraints:

- **Quality**: All deliverables (products) are of acceptable quality.

- **Benefits**: Fixed for minimum viable product (MVP), otherwise flexed.

- **Risk**: Whether fixed or flexed is determined for each project.

Focus areas of control

Constraints and tolerances are agreed at the start of a project and then continually managed through a number of focus areas.

1 **Business case:** The desirability, feasibility, and viability of the project – adaptability is achieved by focusing on the benefits and allowing the deliverables to vary.

2 **Organization:** All projects benefit from clearly defined roles and responsibilities – on agile projects, however, there is more emphasis on decision-making by the team.

3 **Quality:** Every project defines its tolerances around quality – agile projects take a stronger stance, with the bywords **never compromise on quality**.

4 **Plans:** Planning at the start of a project enables the initial stages to be more successful – on agile projects, early planning is at a much higher level, with detailed planning typically left until much closer to the work being done.

5 **Risk:** Projects need to identify, assess, and actively manage their risks and dependencies – on agile projects, this is typically a shared responsibility rather than sitting with the project manager, and recorded on a general risk and impediments board rather than on a separate risk register.

6 **Change:** Due to the additional controls on projects, change has to be approached more carefully – by negotiating what scope can be removed and still achieves the benefits, albeit with greater attention to documenting and tracking such changes.

7 **Progress:** Projects in controlled environments are centered on defining and tracking delivery of each **product** – enabling progress to be treated as per the agile principle of *releasable product is the primary measure of progress*.

The next section explains the principles, and the pages that follow outline the roles and processes that implement them.

Most organizations struggle with how to delegate more responsibility to teams while still retaining control.

Principles of agile control

These principles are intended to guide good practice, and are considered essential in order to class the project as controlled:

Continued business justification

The business case must be continually updated at every stage to ensure the project is still viable, and the project should be terminated early if it is determined to be no longer viable.

Agile projects have to approach justification differently. For a start, forecasting is harder when the product is not fully specified up-front. However, it is easier to track the enablement of benefits through frequent releases. This encourages the use of techniques like **minimum viable product** (MVP) to deliver as little as possible while still generating good outcomes.

Learn from experience

All projects should continually observe and learn to make improvements, both on their own project and for other projects, to avoid repeating the same problems. There's no real difference in this principle for agile projects vs traditional ones, except that agile teams usually take this principle more seriously.

Almost all agile frameworks employ retrospectives as a key technique. They help teams learn from the past, with a focus on recent activities.

Defined roles and responsibilities

Everyone should be able to see who is responsible for what on the project. Implementing this principle should be more lightweight on agile projects.

Where possible, map controlling roles to existing roles in the chosen agile delivery framework. Although these will typically be simpler, it's better to invest the time to streamline rather than cause confusion.

Manage by stages

The project needs to be planned and controlled on a stage-by-stage basis – enabling better focus, and updating plans and the business case between stages. On agile projects, the stages are a repeating cycle of delivery activity. While it is possible for a stage to consist of multiple releases, each made up of the work from several iterations, it is simpler to associate the stage with a release, and this is often based on the **quarterly review and planning** cycle.

Manage by exception

The project board should be continually aware of progress and intervene when a constraint strays outside tolerance.

On agile projects, this principle is strengthened, so the delivery teams are self-organizing too. Enough authority should be given to speed up decision-making and ensure projects don't get blocked.

Focus on products

All the project's deliverables are termed as **products** – each with their own **product definition** that defines its name, purpose, composition, source, skills required, and quality criteria.

The solution is decomposed through a **product breakdown**, and this is used to determine what work gets done, rather than a plan derived from a more traditional work breakdown.

For agile projects, this translates very well to building a prioritized product backlog, with each product as an **epic**, then decomposing these into multiple **stories** (see page 54).

Tailor to suit the project environment

The size, complexity, importance, timeline and risk of the project should be assessed during start-up so that the approach can be tailored to suit. This chapter shows how to tailor for agile projects.

Additional desirable agile behaviors

- **Transparency**: One of the three pillars of empirical thinking (see page 36), transparency brings clarity and openness, even when the news is not so good. Making progress easily visible is critical, such as burn-down charts on an office wall.

- **Rich communication**: Preference is for face-to-face communication (even when remote) or a persistent chat tool, rather than flooding people with email updates.

- **Collaboration**: Motivation and mutual respect are essential for the collaboration that leads to high-performing teams.

- **Self-organization**: As far as possible, keep decision-making with the people doing the work.

- **Continual discovery**: On agile projects, it's important to minimize early commitment by continuing to explore options through discovery workshops, spiking, proofs of concept, etc.

In a controlled project, a *product* is any deliverable, including: the *working solution* itself, any *temporary artifacts* created along the way, and all *management plans and reports*.

Roles and responsibilities

Due to the controlled nature of these environments, there are more formal roles and responsibilities than would normally be seen on agile projects.

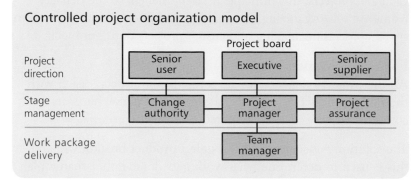

The project organization model is structured on three levels, which correspond to the three process levels (see page 150).

Project direction

At the project direction level sits the project board, usually made up of senior users, an executive, and a senior supplier.

They are accountable to the executive for the success of the project, with the authority to agree on the tolerance settings and direct the project manager when required.

- **Executive:** The executive is ultimately accountable for the project achieving its stated benefits through its business case, and acts as the ultimate decision maker.

- **Senior user:** The senior user or customer representative is responsible for clarifying requirements, acting as a liaison, and for ensuring that the solution meets those requirements. On agile projects, this role may be known as customer representative or even product owner.

- **Senior supplier:** The senior supplier represents the interests of those designing, developing, facilitating, procuring, and implementing the project product. For example, this role may be played by an enterprise architect or development manager.

On agile projects, the project board should understand the principles of agility and be willing to delegate decision-making.

Don't forget

Roles are distinct from people. Someone may play more than one role or may share a role with someone else.

Stage management

At the stage management level sits the project manager.

- **Project manager:** The project manager is accountable to the project board and has the authority to ensure the project produces the required products within the agreed tolerance settings for time, cost, quality, scope, benefits, and risk.

- **Project assurance:** Traditionally, project assurance confirms whether the project is being managed well and the products being delivered are of suitable quality. On agile projects, the first responsibility is typically played by a coach, who helps guide the project rather than auditing for compliance. The responsibility for quality now sits with the whole team.

- **Change authority:** On traditional projects, making changes can be expensive, so changes are restricted, and the change authority is anyone who considers changes. On agile projects, this falls to the product owner and the team to resolve.

Work package delivery

At the work package delivery level sits the delivery team.

- **Self-organizing team:** Although agile principles say that delivery teams should be empowered and self-organized, this is not fully possible within controlled environments. However, we should still give more authority to the teams, which is fully supported by the principle of *manage by exception*.

- **Team manager:** In formal controlled projects, the team manager normally leads the delivery team, so represents those delivering the work package at the project level. On agile projects, however, this is usually delegated to a role like the product owner, who would be accountable for work packages.

Miscellaneous roles

In addition to these nominated roles, there are often subject-matter experts (SMEs) assigned to the project who may represent specific customer groups, distinct technical domains, or other areas of the organization – especially related to how the solution will be used once it has been deployed and operationalized.

In addition, the delivery framework will normally include distinct roles too, like scrum master and product owner (see page 185).

The controlled life-cycle

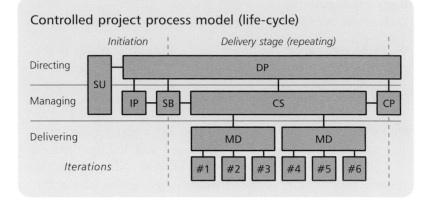

Controlled project process model (life-cycle)

Seven processes oversee the life-cycle of a controlled project:

- **Starting up a project** (SU): The project board and team are appointed, and a project brief is produced.

- **Directing a project** (DP): The project board (steering committee) provides governance and direction to the project.

- **Initiating a project** (IP): Business case and project initiation documents are assembled, including product descriptions.

- **Managing stage boundaries** (SB): Confirms when the project is ready to move to the next stage (on every stage boundary).

  - On agile projects, stage boundaries are planned around one or more releases (work packages), often quarterly.

- **Controlling a stage** (CS): Overseeing work within each stage, including how work packages are defined and distributed.

  - As with other agile project frameworks, discovery and delivery are continual rather than being separate stages.

- **Managing delivery** (MD): The link between the project manager and team manager – embodied in the receipt, execution, delivery, and acceptance of work packages.

  - On agile projects, the delivery team's iterations are managed under this process – with one or more iterations normally required to complete a work package.

- **Closing a project** (CP): The formal decommissioning of the project, with follow-on actions and evaluation of the benefits.

Starting controlled projects

The **start-up** process helps confirm that a project is viable and worthwhile, before committing to initiation:

1 Prepare an outline business case and project brief.

2 Appoint the project board, project manager, and team.

3 Plan the initiation stage and define an approach for delivery and benefits management.

4 Document the tolerances agreed for each of the six project constraints.

Once these steps are completed, the project manager will ask the project board to initiate the project (see page 152). Providing these start-up deliverables will enable the board to confirm whether the project is strategically aligned and should continue.

Variations for agile projects

On agile projects, the **start-up** and **initiation** stages are often combined and called *chartering* or *visioning*, and will normally include some early discovery activities (see Chapter 4).

The **project initiation document** and **initial plan** will be more lightweight than for a more formal plan-driven project in a controlled environment. This is because the repeating cycles of stages, work packages, and iterations mean that discovery and feasibility will evolve throughout the project.

While the level of formality is significantly reduced on agile projects, control artifacts are still needed to answer questions of what, when, and how much. However, the format will vary, such as intranet Wiki pages, project boards, backlogs, and release burn-up charts.

At this stage, requirements will often be captured as bullet points on the **product descriptions**, to be refined later into a backlog.

However, if early discovery workshops are also conducted during initiation, then requirements are more likely to be documented into the backlog as **epics** – high-level descriptions of major capabilities. The quality criteria expected in product descriptions would then be replaced by **acceptance criteria** on those epics.

Requirements may start as *epics* in the backlog or just bullet points in *product descriptions*.

Directing the project

The **directing a project** process describes the responsibilities of the project board, principally overseeing success for the project and ensuring the benefits and business value of the project are realized.

These activities include approving the project to start (through forming the team and initiating the project) and agreeing on the right tolerances for the project's constraints, including whether it is appropriate for it to be run as an agile project.

They provide oversight and guidance to the project and, when required, take over accountability for the success of the project by making key decisions and exercising overall control. However, this is intended to be rare, in response to any major risks or impediments being escalated to them from the project. Otherwise, everything is fully delegated to the project manager and the team.

Communication on agile projects

On agile projects, the degree of formal communication is significantly reduced, with a greater focus on in-person and self-service transparency.

Instead of waiting to receive lengthy progress reports, the project board is expected to show up to iteration reviews, to understand what has been completed and what the teams plan to do next. They are also able to provide feedback at this point as to how well the requirements have been met, or whether there is anything new to be considered.

Overlap with product ownership

The project board's responsibilities around ensuring benefits and business value from the project have some significant overlap with the role of product owner or customer representative. It is, therefore, a good idea for the project board to have a good understanding of product ownership.

On larger projects with multiple delivery teams and product owners, the executive or customer representative on the project board may act as a chief product owner, providing guidance and oversight to the product owners.

Care should be taken to manage the tension between these responsibilities and avoid obvious conflict. The principle of management by exception helps, so that the focus at project-board level is on the high-level aspects.

Controlling stages

The **controlling a stage** process covers how the project plans the work to be done, monitors its delivery, interacts with the project board, deals with risks and impediments, and takes corrective actions when these take the project outside its tolerances.

A stage is itself a timebox with one or more releases or work packages, which are in turn delivered by one or more iterations.

On agile projects, it is common for stages to be planned and managed as three-month increments so that they align with **quarterly review and planning** (QRP) cycles.

The work package

The work to be completed in the quarter is documented for each team as a work package, listing the products they will deliver.

On agile projects, the potential content of work packages is negotiated through collaboration. The product owner or customer representative requests the features they think will be useful for that quarter. The delivery team have the opportunity to query the work package to understand and consider what technically might be required and whether there are any dependencies. The work package is still relatively high-level, as the detailed breakdown will take place closer to the work being done.

Stage boundaries

As each stage ends, the **managing stage boundaries** process covers how the project should review what has been delivered so far with the project board and gain agreement to move to the next stage.

On agile projects, this is often at the QRP event, where the project board and team come together to:

- Review the success of the ending stage.

- Plan the work for the next stage.

- Confirm ongoing business justification and risk levels.

- Approve the next-stage plan.

To avoid interrupting workflow, these end-stage checkpoints are normally conducted like a large-scale review for the whole stage.

The final stage will culminate in the closing of the project, as described on page 155.

Managing product delivery

The **managing product delivery** process helps to orchestrate and synchronize the flow of work and activities between the project and its delivery teams.

Under controlled projects, the delivery team are normally led by a team manager. They formally handle receipt of work packages from the project manager and then assign work within the team to be completed by the end of the stage.

As agile teams do not typically have the role of team manager, this responsibility sits with the product owner or equivalent role. They are accountable for the benefits defined in the work package.

Product delivery on controlled agile projects could use any of the frameworks outlined in Chapter 13, although the timeboxed variants are more suited than the flow-based Kanban method.

Accepting the work package

Under controlled projects, the team manager accepts each work package on behalf of the team, then creates a team plan, assigning activities to team members.

On agile projects, the product owner and delivery team collaborate to agree on what is feasible within the stage, and define the work package based on that.

Executing the work package

Once the team have decomposed the work package into backlog items, they continue to refine them to be ready for each iteration.

During each iteration, they will then progressively work through their iteration plan, completing the items toward completing their work packages. As they complete their work, they update the backlog and any progress charts, like the iteration burn-down.

Delivering the work package

At the end of each iteration, the project board and project team will gather to review the work completed by the delivery team, although it should be noted that the work may not be operationalized until the full work package is completed.

On completion of the whole work package, there will likely be another opportunity to review and approve the completed work so that it can be released to market or operationalized.

Closing controlled projects

As progress is monitored (see page 153), it will become clear when sufficient work packages have been delivered to start the **closing a project** process. This is the final checkpoint to confirm that the project has delivered on its objectives and can be closed.

1 Prepare planned closure.

2 Hand products over to be operationalized.

3 Evaluate the project's delivery against its objectives.

Formal closure is agreed with the project board, unless the project board has intervened to terminate the project early.

End of controlled agile projects

This stage will be lighter for agile projects, as the products should have been deployed and operationalized progressively through each iteration, or at least at the completion of each work package.

If not completed earlier, each product description is checked to:

● Validate that the acceptance criteria have been met.

● Verify that the product has been delivered and operationalized.

● Check that the project has delivered what is expected.

Typical final products at closure

There is always some final paperwork to produce, and while the form of these documents might differ, they are still needed on agile projects.

● **Lessons-learned report**: In line with the *learn from experience* principle, this summarizes lessons learned in the project.

● **Follow-on actions**: Recommendations for those responsible for the ongoing operation and support of the products.

● **Benefits management approach**: Update the project initiation document to reflect which benefits were enabled, how they will be measured and by whom, and when the benefits realization review should be scheduled.

● **End-project report**: A final report on the performance and efficacy of the project.

Summary

- Projects in heavily regulated environments have additional overheads, which does make it harder to run them as agile projects, but not impossible.

- Government agencies created formalized project frameworks that their suppliers had to conform with to continue working with them.

- Projects in Controlled Environments (PRINCE) was one of these, and it has since evolved to work better with agile projects, with PRINCE2 Agile.

- In addition to the original triple constraints of time, cost, and scope, the requirements of working within controlled environments added quality, benefits, and risk.

- These constraints are underpinned by the principles of: continued project justification, learning from experience, clearly defined roles, controlling work in stages, managing by exception, focusing on products, and tailoring the approach.

- The governance overhead is seen in some additional roles typically associated with traditional projects, like the project board, a change authority, and project assurance.

- The life-cycle similarly seeks to include separate processes for each of the governance layers of directing, managing, and delivering.

- Starting up and closing down controlled projects is done in a similar way to most of the other frameworks.

- Directing the project deals with how the project board approve the project to start, agree on tolerances for the project constraints, then provide oversight and guidance, and, by exception, intervene when required.

- Controlling stages deals with defining and handing off work packages to delivery teams, then confirming everything has been done before moving on to the next stage.

- Managing product delivery then deals with how delivery teams accept the work packages, work on them over a number of iterations, and then deliver them when completed.

11 From projects to continual flow

As the business world gears up for a continual flow of value, this chapter explores how to adapt the project management mindset for when there are no more projects.

The shift to continual flow

Projects have served us well as a way of bringing a group of skilled people together, with the joint focus of delivering organization and technical change to achieve defined benefits. However, by definition, projects are temporary organization structures created to achieve those benefits and then dissolved once those benefits have been enabled.

As organizations face up to the need to become increasingly adaptive, many are finding that using projects as the only way to deliver value is limiting.

● There is a time-and-cost overhead every time a new project needs to be approved, a new team formed, and all the preparation completed so that work can start. Similarly, the closure of projects takes time and money to complete.

● An even bigger impediment is that the project team is only there to create business capabilities and get them into operation. When those using the capabilities find something needs to be changed, there is nobody who can act on that.

Instead, requested enhancements get added to a pipeline with other potential work, which has to be prioritized against any other. There is often a time lag until people agree to initiate a project to make that enhancement – if it ever happens.

The shift to product thinking

To realize a return on investment (ROI) for the development and launch of new products, organizations need people to support the product, fixing it when broken and enhancing it to stay relevant. A product is likely to fail if the team move on to developing the next new product and do not support what has been launched.

More and more organizations are starting to treat their business capabilities as if they were products, and this requires them to rethink some fundamental factors of organization design.

The rise of continual flow

In Chapter 2, we learned how the Standish Group conducted extensive research into project management and published their findings in the biannual CHAOS reports. In their 2020 report they reflected on how the profession had evolved over the previous 60 years, and considered what was coming next (see page 22). They forecasted more of a shift from agile to continual flow.

Although still a relatively novel concept, continual flow is no longer just an innovative trend. It has firmly reached the stage of early adoption in forward-thinking organizations, hence its inclusion as a viable alternative agile framework.

Principles of continual flow

Shifting to **continual flow** should eliminate the overhead of managing work through projects, and decrease development costs by as much as 90%.

To make this work, organizations will have to fundamentally redesign themselves to align and work through **value streams**, by:

Geoffrey Moore described the stages of adoption in his book, *Crossing the Chasm*, where the hardest shift is from *early adopters* to the *early majority.*

1 Being clear on who their customers are, what they value, and the capabilities required to deliver that value.

2 Identifying the competencies and capacity to create, support, operate, and eventually replace those capabilities.

3 Forming fully cross-functional long-standing teams of business, development, and operations people.

4 Funding the value stream out of an operational budget.

5 Discovering, prioritizing, developing, and operationalizing that value stream's capabilities as a continual flow of work.

The rest of this chapter details these steps and shows how this shifts change to be incremental rather than big-bang and episodic.

Is this the end for project management?

Although job titles might change, project management skills are essential for success in delivering value via continual flow. We are seeing the emergence of **delivery lead** in place of project manager.

This lays foundations for the evolution of the traditional project management office into the **value management office** (see pages 204-205).

Projects will continue to serve organizations by delivering on outcomes that don't need long-standing teams. There will always be a need for one-off initiatives such as infrastructure builds or major enhancements that require additional capacity.

Value stream design

To enable the transition to continual flow in value streams and sustain it successfully, we need to make careful and deliberate choices. Our structure, work flow, roles, policies, and systems have a significant impact on our outcomes.

Principles of organizational design

Organizational design provides a set of principles that help us consider the internal and external factors that influence our design choices, to enable our organization to be aligned with its current context as well as being equipped to evolve.

Each principle represents a range of options, and the setting chosen for each helps create an appropriate blueprint:

- **Specialization**: Which functions have to be isolated.

- **Orchestration**: Which activities are highly codependent.

- **Delegation**: Which responsibilities can be delegated.

- **Autonomy**: Degree of trust in engagement and commitment.

- **Adaptation**: Degree of readiness needed for ongoing change.

Organizational design for value streams

Large organizations tend to lean toward more mechanistic ways of managing. They want a stable environment so that they can focus on efficiency and performance. However, to make value streams work at scale, we essentially have to descale the organization.

This means redesigning the organization around self-contained units, based on streams of activity that deliver value to identifiable customers. Ideally, each value stream should be established as a distinct line of business, with profit-and-loss accountability.

As far as possible, each value stream should contain all capabilities, competencies, and capacity required to build and operate by itself. To mitigate the risk that this could just replace old functional silos with new product ones, **value stream design** builds on the matrix model of project teams. People are drawn from practices into cross-functional teams, working with dual reporting lines.

For the few highly specialized functions – like finance or legal – it can make sense to assemble them into internal value streams, where the customer is effectively the other value stream.

Don't forget

Any functions needed only occasionally or with very low capacity will also need to act as a shared service like the specialized teams.

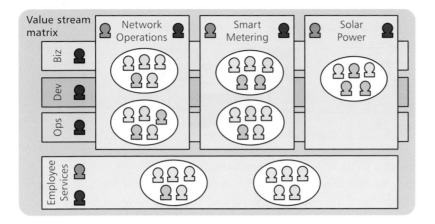

Business, development, and operations

Early moves toward continual flow saw the teams that developed capabilities becoming responsible for operating them (often known as **dev-ops**). This improved ownership and quality.

However, to create fully autonomous value streams, the model had to go further. The roles that actually generate value need to sit alongside those that develop and operate the capabilities (i.e. seating **biz** with **dev** and **ops** above). This reduces decision latency.

The cross-functional teams in these value streams should ideally be long-standing, providing a degree of certainty. However, the reality is that career choices and organization priorities change, so the placement and size of teams will change over time.

Roles in value streams

Most existing roles will stay the same under this new operating model. However, there are some distinct roles called for:

- **Value stream lead** (green heads in the diagram above): Similar to a general manager, accountable for the profit and loss of the value stream – often with a team of product owners.

- **Delivery lead** (pink heads): Similar to a project manager, accountable for negotiating enough capacity to form teams and then facilitating how the teams work – often with a team of scrum masters or team facilitators reporting to them.

- **Practice lead** (blue heads): Similar to a functional line manager – looks after recruitment, pay, people care, training, leave, and supporting placement into value streams.

Beware

To avoid too much disruption, team changes should be limited to once per quarter, timed to coincide with the quarterly review and planning cycle.

Continual flow life-cycle

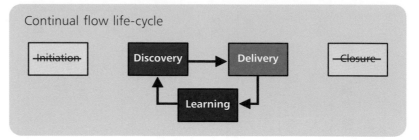

Once a value stream has been established and its teams have been formed, the life-cycle loses the overheads of **initiation** and **closure**. The loop of **discovery**, **delivery**, and **learning** now continues for the life of the value stream.

To help with alignment across the organization, value streams still benefit from taking part in the quarterly review and planning cycle (see illustration below). This enables dependencies between value streams to be identified and removed, or orchestrated around. Thereafter, each value stream should be largely self-regulating.

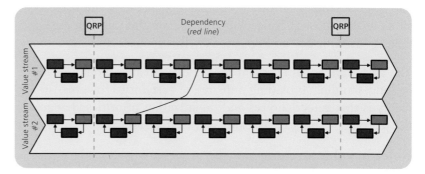

The responsibilities for outcomes, timeframes, scope, and budget now shift from a project basis to an operational gearing. These changes are explored over the following pages.

Describing this as *continual flow* implies this is simply an extension of lean project management; however, there is more to it.

The type of work should dictate the approach. Some work could be handled as a flow of independent items, while other work may be better handled in small batches. For example, value streams may be based on Kanban (see pages 186-187) or Scrum (see pages 184-185).

Larger value streams with multiple teams may find that some of their teams follow different approaches (see pages 206-207).

Shifting out of timeframes

As discussed earlier, a distinctive attribute of projects is that they have a finite timeframe. The team are brought together to build and deliver something and are then disbanded. This makes sense for a one-off infrastructure build, as there is a clear end to the work – the thing has been built, so now it can be used.

However, with internal capabilities and software products there is no definitive end. Instead, these have a life-cycle:

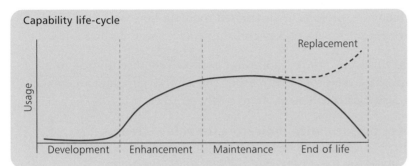

Hot tip

This life-cycle is based on the marketing model for a product life-cycle.

163

- **Development**: Every capability has its origins in discovery and delivery, to the point of becoming operationalized – this may have started as a project before transitioning to a value stream.

- **Enhancement**: Once operationalized, the capability will need problems fixed and enhancements made – usage will increase.

- **Maintenance**: Once the capability is stable and everyone is happy with it, investment will reduce – usage will be stable.

- **End of life**: Usage will decline when people no longer need the capability to generate value in their value stream – once it falls below a certain level, the capability will be switched off.

- **Replacement**: Alternatively, when the needs of the value stream have changed sufficiently, the capability will be replaced – kicking off a whole new life-cycle.

Throughout each of these life-cycle stages, the value stream teams will be repeating the activities of discovery, delivery, and learning.

Where a team are responsible for multiple capabilities, they will likely use a combination of an iterative approach – for capabilities they are developing or enhancing – and a flow approach – for capabilities in maintenance or end of life.

Don't forget

The hybrid approach, *Scrumban*, is discussed on page 183.

Defining success

The way we define success and monitor it dictates how we think about it and our behavior in delivering it.

Defining success for projects

Most business cases build their justification on a promise to deliver benefits that contribute to strategic goals. However, it is not uncommon for the benefits realization review to be scheduled too early to have sufficient information, or to be unable to distinguish the impact it has had, or even to not happen at all.

Therefore, projects are measured more on how well they keep within tolerances on key constraints (see pages 12 and 144).

In this world, the organization is effectively incentivized to overload the project with every conceivable requirement, which usually leads to longer, more costly projects.

Key performance indicators for value streams

In value streams, on the other hand, everyone is responsible collectively for developing and operating capabilities as well as generating value from them. This naturally leads to a set of measures that are more business-focused, such as:

- How many customers does the value stream need to attract?

- At what cost point is this profitable?

- What throughput does the value stream need?

As development and operations share these same key performance indicators, everything they do has to align to achieving them.

Objectives and key results for value streams

Any suggestions for how to improve value stream performance should clearly link the envisaged change with its impact and how it would be measured. An effective way of describing changes and their impact is through objectives and key results (OKRs):

- **Objectives**: Describe overall impact, such as "grow the customer base" or "improve profit margin".

- **Key results**: Show what the impact looks like, such as:

  - An article published should result in 500 new subscribers.

  - A discount should convert 5% of subscribers to customers.

Budgeting

In the project world, the business case includes a forecast of costs and a justification for funding. Once secured, the team can be formed and work can start. Sometimes, the entire funding is given up-front, but more commonly it is tied to project milestones. Although the budget has already been approved, the project still needs to request release of funds as it completes each milestone.

Additional funding could also be required when new scope is discovered or if work overruns. This continual requesting and approving of funds, with associated paperwork and meetings, adds further overhead and inefficiency.

Budgeting for value streams

Investment zones	Disrupting	Sustaining
Revenue performance	**TRANSFORMATION** *Make a big change*	**PERFORMANCE** *Make the top line*
Enabling investments	**INCUBATION** *Create options for the future*	**PRODUCTIVITY** *Make the bottom line*

In value streams, budgets are decided based on how well the value stream is performing, the life-cycle stage of its capabilities, and the spread of investment appetite for incubation, transformation, performance, or productivity (see **investment zones** above).

When an organization needs more from a value stream, it may shift funding from other value streams. This could lead to disbanding teams and forming new ones. However, it would be better to minimize disruption by moving a team together.

Reviewing and setting the budget is part of the **quarterly review and planning** cycle. Even in organizations that still need to agree their indicative high-level budget annually, they will review and adjust the budget on a rolling quarterly basis.

So long as the value stream delivers to its agreed outcomes and performance levels, the value stream lead gets to decide how to invest that budget. This removes much of the overhead of repeated round trips to governance groups for funding approval and release.

Wherever possible, keep teams intact, to avoid disrupting performance, and limit changes to quarterly.

Prioritization

In traditional projects, the scope is typically defined at the outset, and priorities are driven by the project plan.

For most agile projects, scope is agreed early on at a high level only, then confirmed at a detailed level in small batches closer to doing the work. This retains the option to change priorities or introduce new scope without discarding significant investment in analysis and design.

For agile projects using a lean delivery approach, the commitment to scope is typically much shorter – with replenishment required as often as weekly, daily, or even on-demand.

Under continual flow, value streams will use a blend of approaches depending on the type of work. However, it also has to take into account the spread of investment required by the value stream – a concern that most other projects leave to the governance process.

The importance of understanding the type of work

As discussed earlier (see page 165), when setting a budget for the value stream, the organization needs to determine its investment appetite across the four investment zones.

As new work is discovered and added to the backlog, it should be tagged to one of these investment zones so that prioritization can maintain the right balance of investment.

The actual types of work items should be determined by the purpose of each value stream. For the purposes of explaining how this works, the following generic types are used:

- **Value stream requests**: Items that a customer pulls through the value stream – this is how value is generated, so they are typically tagged under performance.

- **New capabilities**: Significant investments to create capabilities or replace existing ones at end of life – typically tagged for transformation, although could also be under incubation.

- **Enhancements**: Smaller investments to improve and adapt a capability – can be tagged to any investment type, depending on the life-cycle stage of the capability.

- **Fixes**: Something that affects the customer or a dysfunction revealed in the metrics – typically tagged for productivity.

Balance investment by zones

In tagging work items to investment zones, we are seeking to ensure we don't over- or undercommit.

For example, a mature value stream would have relatively stable capabilities, and so should be concerned that customers don't leave faster than new ones join, and that the team keep their cost base as low as possible. Their likely balance could be 10% incubation, 10% transformation, 20% performance, and 60% productivity.

That would mean if they had already committed 10% of their budget to incubating new ideas, they should wait until the following quarter before considering any more.

Competition between investment zones

Sometimes this can lead to critical work not getting done in time, so the value stream should also determine its relative weighting between the types of investment. This is usually highly dependent on where the value stream itself is in its life-cycle.

- **Start-up value streams**: The emphasis will be on testing new ideas to see what customers value and how they could be delivered profitably. Precedence should be given to incubation, then transformation, performance, and productivity.

- **Launching value streams**: The emphasis will be on strengthening and developing capabilities. This means precedence should be given to transformation, then incubation, performance, and productivity.

- **Growing value streams**: More emphasis will be given to expanding the customer base and growing sales. Precedence should be given to performance, then productivity, transformation, and incubation.

- **Mature value streams**: The emphasis switches to retaining customers and getting the maximum out of stable capabilities. Now, precedence should be given to productivity, then performance, transformation, and incubation.

- **End-of-life value streams**: Finally, the emphasis will be on renewing and replacing old capabilities to reenergize the value stream, or maybe on how to exit the market. Precedence would now likely switch to behaving like a start-up again.

Risk management

Traditionally, project risks are handled by attempting to identify them all and planning for mitigation and resolution. Knowing that we cannot identify all risks up-front, however, the timeframe and budget tend to be expanded with contingency. While this may be appropriate for a one-off implementation that follows a tried-and-tested approach, projects are increasingly complex (see Chapter 1).

We know from the Cynefin model (see page 10) that complex problems need exploratory solutions, which is the reason we have agile project frameworks. However, in terms of planning, we often see an additional iteration or two added as contingency.

In value streams using continual flow, risk is spread across the whole life-cycle and multiple iterations. This creates opportunities to adjust aspects of the capability if initial hypotheses are incorrect or new opportunities arise.

Minimum viable product

By adopting lean start-up and product thinking, value streams can minimize risk by working to a **minimum viable product** (MVP).

This means delivering an early version of a capability with just enough features to provide some value. Eliciting feedback can then identify further development, including the potential to **pivot** or change direction if they have completely missed the mark. This focuses the team on what really creates impact and avoids lengthy and unnecessary work.

Risks by life-cycle stage

The way risk is handled depends on the capability life-cycle stage:

- In the **development** stage, we adopt a hypothesis-driven development approach, like the MVP described above.

- Once operationalized and in **enhancement**, we ensure changes are incremental and made in small batches.

- In the **maintenance** stage, risk should be lower and minimized by handling changes as a flow of individual items.

- At **end of life**, we focus on organizational change, potentially in parallel with the development stage of a **replacement**.

In all other regards, the approach to assessing and managing risks is the same as with other agile frameworks (see page 34).

Transparency in continual flow

As with all frameworks for agile projects (see Chapters 8-10 and 12) and agile delivery (see Chapter 13), transparency is critical to:

- Know we are working on the right things.

- See how well things are progressing.

- Learn how we can do things better.

However, many of the charts explored elsewhere in the book assume we know enough to be able to chart progress toward a known end point, like the release burn-up (see page 37).

Under continual flow, however, we are continually prioritizing and adapting, meaning scope could be changing multiple times per day. The focus for transparency therefore has to shift more to how work flows through the value stream.

Continual flow metrics

These five metrics indicate how well a value stream is performing, and provide insights into where improvements can be made:

- **Flow velocity**: The count of items of each type completed over a set period of time – indicates pace of delivery.

- **Flow time**: The time it takes for items of each type to go from in progress to done (similar to cycle time), including active time and wait time – indicates time to value.

- **Flow efficiency**: The ratio of active time to wait time compared to the total flow time for each type – indicates potential bottlenecks or waste in the value stream process.

- **Flow load**: The count of items of each type in progress at the any one time – indicates over- or under-utilization of the value stream and potentially unsustainable work practices.

- **Flow distribution**: The ratio of the count of items of each type completed over a set period of time – indicates whether actual effort matches the chosen spread of investment zones.

Other metrics for value streams

These metrics are in addition to the key performance indicators that reflect the value stream's business performance, and the objectives and key results that reflect any high-level improvements planned to how the value stream operates (see page 164).

Summary

- As the business world moves more to a value stream organizational design, there is growing recognition that it is no longer served by the overhead of running projects as a temporary vehicle to deliver value.

- Continual flow combines many elements of lean processes and thinking without the need to initiate and close projects.

- Value stream design is a particular organizational design based on applying the matrix team model onto value streams, creating long-standing cross-functional teams.

- These teams need to combine business roles along with development and operational roles too.

- Some distinct new roles have arisen, like the value stream lead who acts as the general manager to the value stream, and the delivery lead who ensures the value stream has the capacity it needs and then facilitates the teams.

- Some project managers are making the transition to the delivery lead role, as this has essentially the same skills as a competent agile project manager.

- The project life-cycle is replaced by a never-ending loop of discovery, delivery, and learning.

- Value streams still need to synchronize with other value streams and programs in the quarterly review and planning cycle – this should identify potential dependencies and either eliminate them or orchestrate around them to reduce risk.

- The value stream capability life-cycle illustrates how the type of work and investment needed depends on whether something is under development, being enhanced, in maintenance, or at end-of-life.

- Value streams need to base how they prioritize and plan work on their investment approach, balanced across the four zones of incubation, transformation, performance, and productivity.

- Continual flow includes the five new metrics of flow velocity, flow time, flow efficiency, flow load, and flow distribution – these indicate how well the value stream is flowing.

12 Agile projects at scale

Overview

Most of the agile methods already covered in this book deal with the people, processes, and technical practices involved with running an agile project with a single team. There is a common perception that agile projects are best suited for small projects working on new software systems with unknown or uncertain requirements where the solution is unclear and are best built incrementally.

Large organizations, however, tend to have legacy systems and other infrastructures to adapt and integrate, to use tens if not hundreds of development teams, and to have many projects running at the same time, all competing for limited money, resources, time, and people.

Once large organizations have successfully deployed one or two systems through agile projects, they naturally want to apply the same practices across all their projects, but find they are limited by practices that were developed for small teams and that typically focus solely on the development stage of a project. This can lead to organizations deciding that their large programmes must still use traditional waterfall practices, often leading to costly overruns.

Unfortunately, many of these organizations are also starting to face greater volatility, uncertainty, and complexity in their markets, increasing competition from overseas, and disruption from new start-up companies that have a cleaner starting point. These 21st-century problems need a more adaptable approach – one that allows them to build or enhance products rapidly and prove them with small numbers of customer, and one that allows them to progressively develop and add new features as they uncover what excites customers. In short, organizations need to run agile projects at scale but many have not, so far, found the tools to do this.

Frameworks for scaling agile projects

Over the last few years, a number of frameworks and patterns have evolved that seek to answer the question of how to successfully use agile practices for all development projects.

- **Lean Governance** is a pattern of lean principles for project governance, combining oversight with light-touch controls.

- The **Agile Project Framework** (APF) is the original framework for agile projects, covering everything from pre-project initiation to post-project closure (see Chapter 8).

Beware

Managing agile projects as part of a waterfall program will usually lead to delays and cost overruns.

- **Projects in Controlled Environments** (PRINCE) is a project framework suited to running projects in regulated industries; however it does support agile at scale too (see Chapter 10).

- **Large-Scale Scrum** (LeSS) is a framework for applying Scrum practices to large projects; two variants of this, **Scrum at Scale** and **Enterprise Scrum**, have also been published.

- **Nexus Scrum** is Scrum.org's framework for applying Scrum practices to large and very large projects.

- The **Scaled Agile Framework** (SAFe) is a pragmatic collection of proven lean and agile product development techniques that help organizations adopt agile at enterprise scale.

- **Disciplined Agile** (DA) is a framework for choosing between iterative and incremental delivery methods (see pages 192-193).

The remainder of this chapter reviews each of these frameworks.

There is ongoing discussion, research, and experimentation within and between the agile practitioner and project management communities to find the best mix of techniques and patterns for agile projects at scale. As covered elsewhere in the book, agile delivery methods are often combined, such as Scrum and XP. So, too, can these frameworks, with APF, be used to manage programs within SAFe, and Lean Governance applied at the portfolio level.

Comparison table

The table below summarizes how well each framework covers significant areas of project concern outside the delivery team. Many of these include patterns or practices that can be combined to tailor the approach for an organization.

Framework	Product	Program	Portfolio	Org
Lean Governance	N	N	Y	Y
Agile Project Framework	Y	Y	N	N
Projects in Controlled Environments	Y	Y	N	N
Large-Scale Scrum	Y	Y	N	N
Nexus	Y	Y	N	N
Scaled Agile Framework	Y	Y	Y	N
Disciplined Agile	Y	Y	N	N

This table compares the frameworks and patterns for operating agile projects at scale.

Governance should be primarily about balancing the selection of initiatives in which to invest with just enough oversight to ensure they deliver what is promised.

Agile in the enterprise

These frameworks for large agile projects encompass the work of people outside the development teams, and particularly those with responsibilities outside the project itself, such as project governance, product management, and portfolio prioritization.

In order to be effective and to ensure that high-performing agile teams are not blocked from delivering, it is important that these frameworks follow patterns and practices that are complementary to those used by the development teams; for example, that major gate reviews should be synchronized with the timing of iterations, or at least to ensure that they take place in a way that doesn't cause interruptions to the teams.

Governance

Governance, loosely, is about two things: The first is to ensure that organizations choose wisely how to invest their limited money, resources, and time, by ensuring that all developments are aligned with strategy. The second is to ensure that what is delivered meets the needs of the customer and of the organization itself. Agile governance strives to ensure these vital concerns are fulfilled without undermining agile development practices.

Product or project perspective

Projects are, by design, temporary vehicles for delivering change. As we saw in Chapter 11, many organizations are switching their focus from running projects to assigning teams that permanently support and enhance a product. In these circumstances, projects become more the means of funding the work than of organizing it. With this shift comes a lighter overhead around initiation and closure, as the team persist beyond the individual project.

Agile portfolio prioritization

In the same way that teams need a backlog of defined and funded work to keep focused and productive, so, too, the organization overall needs a pipeline of potential work. Whenever senior management are asked to consider investing in the next best thing, they need sight of everything else that is already underway and other ideas that are waiting in the wings. They need to be able to respond to changing market conditions, and this could mean postponing planned work or stopping in-flight work. The advantage to organizations following agile practices is that should work be stopped, there will still be something that can be released.

Lean Governance

Stage gates are the key decision points in a governance process by which work is approved to progress from one stage to the next. This leads many to associate gates with waterfall projects and thus consider them undesirable or unnecessary on agile projects. Most enterprises, however, have too many things they would like to do and insufficient money and time to do them, so governance and oversight through gates is vital on agile projects too.

Beware

Over-engineered governance will lead to delays and cost overruns.

As this involves senior executives, the work is often spread across locations and times, making gates a drawn-out multi-step process.

Streamlining the gates

Governance oversight can be made lean and effective. However, this requires the right timing, preparation, tools, and process.

- Sessions are on the same frequency as development iterations.

- All work is visualized: whether new, prioritized, or in progress.

- Executives assess everything against the same criteria; e.g. strategic fit, customer needs, feasibility, cost, profitability, etc.

- New work that fails the criteria is binned or reworked while what passes is prioritized against impact, effort, and urgency.

- Work in progress may be deployed, paused, or canceled to free up funds and resources for higher-priority new work.

Don't forget

Governance can become leaner by keeping reviews simpler, having all information at your fingertips, and ensuring everyone is adequately prepared.

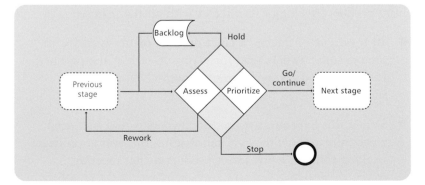

Large-Scale Scrum (LeSS)

In applying Scrum to bigger projects, **Large-Scale Scrum** (LeSS) addresses the issues of scaling by taking a product-based approach, maintaining the product owner's responsibility for their product and resolving how they work effectively with several teams together toward a single shippable increment every sprint.

What changes in Large-Scale Scrum

The essence of the framework is still Scrum. However, there are some additional roles and events to cope with coordinating the work of so many people. Critically, new events should still be timeboxed and take no longer than if they were for a single team.

- The two parts of iteration planning are formally separated. In the first half, representatives from all scrum teams select the backlog items they'll work on in the coming sprint. In the second half, each team works independently to break the committed backlog items into tasks.

- Daily stand-ups continue as normal, with an additional **town-hall meeting**, or **scrum of scrums**, for team representatives to share information and coordinate on dependent tasks.

- Backlog refinement also splits into two, with a light-touch refinement by team representatives, followed by an in-depth refinement by team members across the project.

- The iteration review should include everyone involved from the teams, as well as stakeholders, partners, and third parties.

- Retrospectives are still separate per team, and there is often an additional shared retrospective after all the team retrospectives.

Some products, however, require so much work that a single product owner would struggle to maintain an overview of the entire product backlog or to interact with all the teams.

- In these circumstances, a **chief product owner** works with **area product owners** who focus on sub-sets of the product; each area product owner would, themselves, work with multiple teams, as described above.

- When this happens, the product owners would also need to coordinate how they are subdividing the overall product backlog through a pre-sprint product owner meeting.

Nexus Scrum

The **Nexus Scrum** framework recognizes that developing a new product, or the next release of a product, often takes several teams, which challenges many organizations that suffer from isolated teams, badly integrated products, and delayed releases.

These problems can be mitigated by coordinating work through Nexus – the point of connection for three to nine teams that are working on the same product.

All work for a product should be managed by a single product owner, through a single product backlog. All Nexus teams collaborate on how they pull work from a common backlog and focus on the completion of well-integrated shippable product increments each and every sprint.

An additional role in Nexus
To ensure the level of coordination required, Nexus introduces a new **integration team** that coordinate the work of the Nexus teams. This team operate as a fully cross-functional team themselves, including all disciplines required to coordinate, integrate, and release product increments by the end of each iteration (if not before).

Events in Nexus
Some of the traditional Scrum events are replaced.

● Sprints begin with Nexus iteration planning: combined planning to coordinate the work of all teams, highlighting dependencies and leading to an integrated product increment.

● The Nexus daily stand-up, equivalent to a **scrum of scrums**, for representatives of each team to gather to evaluate progress and impediments, and replan if required.

Nexus is built on Scrum, rather than replacing it
Organizations wanting to operate Scrum at scale must first ensure that they fully understand and practice Scrum well at the team level, focused on delivering potentially shippable increments of quality product every sprint, and continually improving by inspecting and adapting.

Successful organizations will focus and measure themselves more on value delivered, time to market, and ability to innovate than on rigid adherence to cost, time, scope, and quality compliance.

Scaled Agile Framework (SAFe)

The **Scaled Agile Framework** (SAFe) applies lean and agile principles at all levels of the project world: portfolio, program, project, and delivery teams. SAFe is freely available, which has helped it to become the most frequently and widely implemented framework for operating agile projects at enterprise scale.

The key model in the framework is the **big picture** (simplified version below), which summarizes the key roles, processes, and artifacts, and how they interrelate. Note: the full diagram is available for free on the website **www.scaledagileframework.com**

Hot tip

The *Scaled Agile Framework* has become the leading framework for operating agile projects at scale, as it covers portfolio and program levels as well as delivery teams.

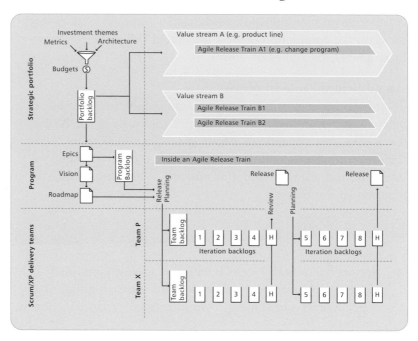

The core elements of SAFe

At the portfolio level, programs are aligned to strategic themes through identified value streams (such as product lines) with a backlog of business and architecture **epics** that can span multiple releases by being broken down into **features** for release planning.

These value streams are implemented through **agile release trains** (equivalent to a program) that provide the tight-knit development organization to define, build, test, and deploy.

Agile release trains (or ARTs) can support up to 15 teams that incrementally build features that are released every five to six iterations. There are other SAFe editions to support more teams.

Roles in SAFe

At the heart of SAFe are the delivery teams, with the same core roles: product owner, scrum master, and up to nine team members.

At the program level: a **product manager** is responsible for the program backlog, roadmap, and coordinating the work of the product owners; a **release train engineer** (a role often filled by an agile project manager) is responsible for program-level processes, impediments, improvements, and coordinating the scrum masters. This is supported by system development/operations, release management teams, and various specialist roles shared across the program, such as user-experience design, architecture, etc.

At the portfolio level: a portfolio management team of senior executives look after high-level financial and product governance.

Practices in SAFe

Delivery teams follow Scrum for self-organizing team practices and Extreme Programming (XP) for code quality and technical principles, which is why SAFe calls them Scrum/XP teams. Iterations at the team level follow the same principles as described elsewhere in the book, progressively developing stories until features are complete enough for a release.

SAFe promotes a continuous deployment approach, releasing products and new features to customers as soon as they are ready. However, SAFe does recognize that in complex operating environments, releases often run on a longer cycle, and it recommends no longer than three months between releases.

Each release starts with release planning, runs through a number of development iterations, and typically ends with a hardening iteration, where the system is stabilized and readied for release. The release is confirmed through a release review, and cross-team improvements are identified through a release retrospective.

The portfolio management team use their agreed investment themes to funnel funding and work to program backlogs for each respective program and its ARTs.

Finally, SAFe also recognizes that even organizations that have fully embraced agile project management often run traditional waterfall programs too. To avoid duplication and redundancy in governance, the SAFe model can operate them all in parallel.

Summary

- Most agile methods focus on individual development teams, failing to address how teams work effectively together.

- Large organizations typically have many development teams across multiple locations, and many legacy systems with which new software has to work seamlessly.

- Any changes to legacy systems are typically managed through traditional waterfall projects, often causing significant delays to the agile projects that are dependent on those changes.

- Senior leadership has to support an agile transformation across the whole enterprise, not just in software development.

- Organizations need to create a joined-up change management approach that caters for all affected areas across the enterprise.

- Project governance has to be modified to oversee agile projects or risk killing them unintentionally at stage gates.

- Senior leadership has to get tougher with its portfolio, limiting the number of in-flight projects, be quicker to cancel lower-return projects in favor of higher priorities, and always look to release value early where possible.

- Organizations benefit from taking a longer-term product management perspective rather than a short-term project one.

- Several frameworks have emerged that help address aspects of this, but none of them addresses every aspect of concern.

- Large-Scale Scrum (LeSS) maintains a product management focus across potentially massively scaled projects.

- Nexus Scrum provides a way of coordinating work across up to nine teams working on the same product.

- The Scaled Agile Framework (SAFe) addresses portfolio and program concerns, as well as the work of teams.

- Disciplined Agile (DA) provides a decision-tree approach to selecting the right agile practices for each project.

13 Frameworks for agile delivery

With preceding chapters covering several frameworks for project management, this chapter looks at compatibility with five key delivery frameworks.

Delivery frameworks

As a book on *agile project management*, the main focus has been on defining a typical agile project life-cycle (see Chapters 3-7) and the project management frameworks that support it (see Chapters 8-12). However, as discussed in Chapter 1, there is also a broad field of complementary delivery frameworks used on agile projects.

This chapter compares and explores the five most popular frameworks:

- **Scrum**: A timebox-driven incremental delivery framework.

- **Kanban method**: A flow-driven delivery framework.

- **Feature-Driven Development** (FDD): A scope-driven incremental delivery framework.

- **Extreme Programming** (XP): A collection of technical practices.

- **Disciplined Agile**: A *build-your-own* approach, picking from all other frameworks, methods, and techniques.

Plug-and-play factors
Each delivery framework has its pros and cons, so it is important to consider the factors that should make it possible to integrate a delivery framework with a project management framework.

When considering which delivery framework to use with a chosen project management framework, the following factors apply:

- **Orientation**: Whether the delivery framework focuses on people and collaboration or more on process and control.

- **Team size**: How large a team each framework supports.

- **Iteration length**: How long the iterations can be.

- **Pros and cons**: The highlights of each framework's strengths and weaknesses.

- **Popularity**: The proportion of teams that report using each framework – note that these add up to more than 100%, because many teams combine frameworks.

- **Framework compatibility**: The project management frameworks and other delivery frameworks each one is known to be compatible with.

Comparison of delivery frameworks

The table below compares four of these delivery frameworks against these factors.

	Scrum	Kanban	FDD	XP
Orientation	People	Process	Process	People
Team size	About 7	N/A	10-50	At least 2
Iteration length	7-30 days	Daily up to 2 weeks	Varies by scope	2-3 weeks
Pros	• Timeboxed • Comms	• Visibility • Flow	• Modeling • Big projects	• Simple • Quality
Cons	• Lack of docs	• Disjointed • No timebox	• Skillset • Not small	• Lack of docs • Code-heavy
Popularity	80%	15%	<2%	37%
Compatibility (project)	All	Lean	DSDM or Lean	All
Compatibility (delivery)	XP, Scrumban	XP, Scrumban	XP	Scrum, XP, Kanban, FDD

This *popularity* is as reported in the annual *State of Agile* survey (digital.ai/resource-center/analyst-reports/state-of-agile-report).

Notes on compatibility

Many of these delivery frameworks are compatible (can plug and play) with one or more agile project management frameworks, and even with other delivery frameworks.

Disciplined Agile (DA), the last framework covered in this chapter, is not included in the table above, as it operates as a library of all techniques and practices. On the one hand, this means it is compatible with all frameworks; on the other, it does require an up-front investment to consider which options would best suit.

Scrumban

The **Scrumban** method (referenced in the table) is a hybrid that combines the structure from *Scrum* with the pull-based flow from *Kanban*. This is typically adopted by teams that have to balance capacity between operational support (for which they use Kanban) and developing new capabilities (for which they use Scrum).

Teams forecast how much capacity is required for operational support, then limit their commitment for new work to what is achievable. Their boards are also hybrid, typically with an expedite swim-lane for operational issues at the top of the board, with the rest of the board working like a typical Scrum team board.

Scrum

Scrum is a framework for managing delivery on iterative and incremental projects. While it is most often used for software development, it is also applicable to other types of projects.

Background

Hirotaka Takeuchi and Ikujiro Nonaka introduced an adaptive product development approach they called *rugby*, to highlight how a team should collaborate like rugby forwards moving down the pitch together, rather than separately like runners in a relay race.

Ken Schwaber and Jeff Sutherland then reimagined this as a software delivery framework they called **Scrum**. In the game of rugby the *scrum* itself is the method of restarting the game after a minor infringement. The Scrum Guide is updated and published every two years and is available at: **www.scrumguides.org**

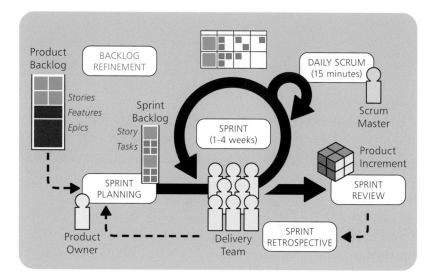

Scrum framework

The framework on which Scrum is based is a small set of loosely defined rules. These rules describe the responsibilities, timings, and deliverables that enable feedback-driven product development. These combine iterative design, incremental development, self-organizing teams, and continual improvement.

Being a framework for delivery means that Scrum complements any of the agile project frameworks (see Chapters 8-12) and a number of techniques for discovery, design, and development – such as Extreme Programming (XP) explored later in this chapter.

The Scrum framework is covered in more depth in our companion book **Scrum in easy steps**.

Scrum fits well with all agile project frameworks.

The Scrum framework consists of the Scrum team (and the roles within it), the events that take place, the artifacts used and produced, and the rules that define how these all interact.

The Scrum team

There are three key roles within the team:

- **Product owner**: Responsible for the business value of the product, selecting *what* gets done and explaining *why*.

- **Team members**: Cross-functional team (i.e. with all the skills required) that self-organize around deciding *how* the work gets done and completing it.

- **Scrum master**: Responsible for ensuring the team are motivated, productive, and following their working agreement.

Events in Scrum

There are five events central to the framework:

- **Sprint**: The *timebox* or *iteration* (normally two weeks) within which all work and the other events take place.

- **Sprint planning**: The team agree on the capabilities for the next sprint with the product owner, then plan the work required.

- **Daily scrum**: The team plan the work for that day and, based on progress and impediments, replan the rest of the sprint.

- **Sprint review**: The team demonstrate the work they completed to their stakeholders and gather their feedback.

- **Sprint retrospective**: The team look back at how the last sprint went and agree on possible team improvement actions.

Scrum artifacts

There are three core artifacts:

- **Product backlog**: A prioritized requirements list of desired capabilities, product features, and other required work.

- **Sprint backlog**: A sub-set of work from the product backlog that the team agree to complete in the next sprint, with tasks.

- **Product increment**: The capabilities and features the team completed in the sprint, added to work already completed.

Successful teams embrace the values on which Scrum is built, as enshrined in the Agile Manifesto (see page 14).

In addition to these events, the team will collaborate with the product owner in discovery and backlog refinement to prepare the product backlog.

Kanban method

Often over-simplified as a visualization of workflow through columns on a board that represent states of work items, **Kanban** (or, more fully, the **Kanban method**) is a workflow management method for incremental, evolutionary delivery and change.

Background
Kanban originated as a scheduling approach in manufacturing, switching production to a pull-based approach and seeking to minimize waste without sacrificing productivity (see also *Agile projects with lean principles*, Chapter 9).

Early agile practitioners developed this into the Kanban method for managing complex knowledge work, such as software development or research and development.

Kanban starts by visualizing the workflow via a board (example shown opposite), then continually adapts this to optimize for both efficiency and effectiveness. The fundamentals can be summarized into two sets of principles and six practices.

Principles of service delivery
As a *service-oriented* workflow management approach, Kanban is based on three principles of service delivery:

- **Customer needs**: Delivery is at the heart of Kanban; by focusing on customer needs, quality and value will follow.

- **Manage the work**: Teams self-organize around the work, enabling a focus on outcomes, and avoid micro-managing.

- **Regularly review**: Continually reinforce the focus on customer, quality, and flow of value, and identify any improvements.

Principles of continual improvement
Kanban also seeks to continually improve, extending these with three principles of continual improvement:

- **Start from where you are**: Preserve processes and roles that work, and focus instead on fixing one issue at a time.

- **Pursue evolutionary change**: Minimize disruption, through a continual process of making small incremental changes.

- **Delegated leadership**: Encourage and model decision-making and problem-solving at all levels, fostering self-organization.

Don't forget

The Japanese word *Kanban* literally means "visual board", and describes how workflow is prominently displayed for all to see.

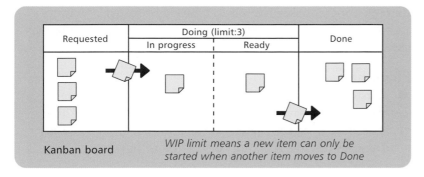

Kanban board

WIP limit means a new item can only be started when another item moves to Done

Practices

- **Visualize the workflow**: Create columns on a board for the states work flows through, with cards to represent work items.

- **Limit work in progress** (WIP): Focus on completing work by teams pulling in work only when they have capacity.

- **Manage flow**: Ensure work can flow through at a predictable and sustainable pace (never starve or block a team).

- **Make policies explicit**: Have clear entry-and-exit criteria, just like the definition of ready (see page 53) and done (see page 81).

- **Feedback loops**: Regular reviews and retrospectives will ensure the quality of work and identify potential improvements.

- **Improve collaboratively**: Collaborate on identifying and making hypothesis-driven and evidence-based improvements.

Meetings

- **Team replenishment**: The team ensure they have enough of the right work and can deliver it; from daily to biweekly.

- **Daily Kanban meeting**: The team "walk the board" daily, to check that WIP limits are being respected and to identify any potential blockers they can swarm around to fix.

- **Team retrospective**: The team review how they work to identify potential improvements; from biweekly to monthly.

- **Service delivery review**: The team and their stakeholders review overall performance in delivering service improvement.

- **Risk review**: To review team-level blockers and identify systemic problems requiring a larger change initiative.

Extreme Programming (XP)

Extreme Programming (XP) is a lightweight software delivery approach based on a number of technical team practices that has proven to be popular in the software development community.

Planning

- **Customer satisfaction**: Rather than delivering everything the customer says they want at some future date, XP aims to deliver what the customer wants as they need it, based on frequent releases and short development timeboxes.

- **Feedback loops**: XP has a number of planning and feedback loops built in; the scope is defined through user stories, which are used to create plans.

- **Release plan**: The team look several months ahead at which stories the customer wants to be released in that time.

- **Iteration plan**: The plan for the next iteration then includes as many of the customer's priority user stories as the team believe they can build for that timebox.

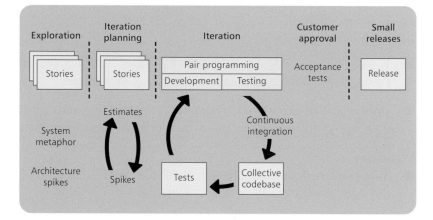

Underlying principles

- **Feedback**: The time between taking an action and its feedback is critical to learning and making changes.

- **Keep it simple**: Avoid developing everything the customer may want; focus on making small changes and release them frequently.

- **Embrace change**: Expecting things to change and be adaptive when they do, incorporating changes into the next release.

XP is based on 12 practices, grouped into four areas:

Fine-scaled feedback

- **Pair programming**: Two people collaborate on a single task – one working on the detail, while the other continually reviews.

- **Planning game**: The team meet once per iteration to refine the backlog and agree on an iteration plan.

- **Test-Driven Development** (TDD): Automated tests defined in advance, and development stops as soon as all tests are passed.

- **Whole team**: The customer or end-user stakeholders should be regarded as part of the team.

Continuous process

- **Small releases**: Delivers value early to the customer, encouraging feedback and reinforcing the concept of whole team.

- **Continuous integration**: Ensures the team always work with up-to-date content, and ensures their work integrates well.

- **Refactoring**: Improving the internal quality of the code without changing the external behavior; e.g. after TDD.

Shared understanding

- **Coding standards**: Ensures a consistent approach and provides a reference for code reviews.

- **Collective ownership**: Whole team are jointly responsible for their work, meaning any of them can fix or change anything.

- **Simple design**: Always check if there is a simpler way to solve the same problem before starting or refactoring code.

- **System metaphor**: Simplifies language by describing the purpose of a solution or its components using everyday words.

Team wellbeing

- **Sustainable pace**: People perform best when they are not overworked, so plan on 30 hours of focused work in a 40-hour week, and do not force overtime over multiple iterations.

While these practices appear very technical, many of them can be repurposed for any type of knowledge work; for example, for *pairing*, a copywriter and legal expert could coauthor a web page.

Always include the customer or business end user in the team.

If you overwork the team for sustained periods, the quality of their work will deteriorate.

Feature-Driven Development

Feature-Driven Development (FDD) is an agile delivery approach with five core processes, six main deliverables, six key roles, and six core practices.

Life-cycle and deliverables

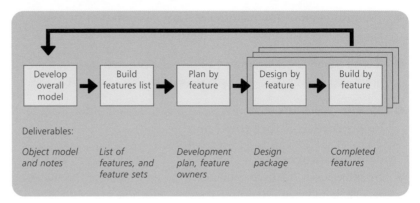

The first three processes are done once per project, or per major release on a large project, and cover defining an overall model, a feature list, and a high-level plan. The last two processes are repeated, iteratively, for each feature as it is progressively designed, developed, and tested.

Where additional information is discovered during design and build, the model should be revisited (indicated by the loopback).

 Develop an overall model: Walk through the scope and define a high-level model for the solution to be delivered.

 Build a features list: Create a list of the key capabilities required, with the state changes and interactions, grouping them into feature sets and subject areas for planning.

 Plan by feature: Agree on an initial schedule and assign responsibilities for each feature or feature set.

 Design by feature: Further develop the model for each feature that defines the detailed requirements.

 Build by feature: Develop and test the solution to the point it can be deployed.

Beware

FDD differs from other agile delivery frameworks, as iteration length flexes to the size of the features, rather than fixing a timebox and breaking features into smaller units.

Practices

There are six practices for successful Feature-Driven Development.

- **Object modeling**: Understanding the problem domain to create a model that acts as a framework for defining features.

- **Feature ownership**: Assigning distinct features (or classes) to a single person, accountable for their consistency and quality.

- **Feature teams**: A dynamically formed team of those working in the same feature set – emphasizes a sense of collective responsibility that helps balance individual ownership.

- **Regular builds**: Building and integrating as often as possible ensures there is always a working solution.

- **Inspections**: Ensuring good-quality design and development through frequent reviews of work.

- **Visibility of progress**: The state of each feature should be clear, with frequent progress reporting of the whole project.

Roles

FDD has six roles, though an individual may have multiple roles:

- **Project manager**: The administrative lead, responsible for budget, head count, and progress reports; also helps maintain focus by acting as a shield to keep away external distractions.

- **Chief architect**: Responsible for overall design, often running design workshops and steering technical decisions.

- **Development manager**: Responsible for coordinating assignments to match capacity to demand.

- **Chief programmer**: An experienced developer – often a team lead; guides developers in deciding feature ownership.

- **Feature owner**: Members of a feature team, including all disciplines; responsible for discrete elements of features.

- **Domain expert**: The stakeholders closest to the requirements, responsible for representing the domain to the feature team.

- **Supporting roles**: Additional roles supporting the teams, including: release management, technical writing, etc.

Disciplined Agile

In contrast with the other frameworks in this chapter, rather than defining a life-cycle or methodology, **Disciplined Agile** (DA) uses the whole field of agile methods and techniques like a library.

DA provides the tools to assess a project's needs then guides through the options so that practitioners can select which methods and techniques are applicable to their context.

Underlying principles
These eight principles for DA are based on lean and agile concepts:

 Delight customers: Go beyond just meeting expectations and needs – strive to delight stakeholders and customers.

 Be awesome: Always focus on doing work with quality and due diligence, then inspect and adapt to get better at it.

 Context counts: Each situation is unique and deserves a way of working that serves the context and the objectives.

 Be pragmatic: Aim to be effective, rather than perfect. No single framework is a silver bullet – use agile, lean, or even traditional strategies when they make the most sense.

 Choice is good: Selecting the right way of working means understanding trade-offs between options.

 Organize around products: Identify value streams and bring all capabilities required to develop and support them.

 Enterprise-aware: Look beyond the needs of the team and work toward the long-term needs of the organization.

 Optimize flow: Adopt ways of working that benefit the value stream rather than favoring an individual team.

DA addresses concerns that many agile delivery frameworks don't cover, such as how architecture fits into the agile life-cycle, and specific topics such as effective documentation, enterprise-wide quality, and agile analysis techniques.

The best overview of Disciplined Agile is provided in the book *Choose your WOW! A Disciplined Agile Approach to Optimizing Your Way of Working* by Mark Lines and Scott Ambler.

Life-cycle

DA supports agile, lean, continuous, and even plan-driven program life-cycles, based on the following generic stages:

● **Inception**: How to get the project going.

● **Construction**: How to incrementally build a working solution.

● **Transition**: How to release the solution into operation.

● **Ongoing**: How to develop and improve ways of working.

Roles

There are five primary roles in Disciplined Agile projects:

● **Stakeholder**: Someone who is materially impacted by the outcome of the solution. More than just an end user or customer, this is anyone potentially affected by the development and deployment of a software project.

● **Product owner**: The person on the team who speaks as the "one voice of the customer", representing the needs of the stakeholder community to the agile delivery team.

● **Team member**: The team member focuses on producing the actual solution for stakeholders, including but not limited to: testing, analysis, architecture, design, programming, planning, and estimation. They will have a sub-set of the overall needed skills and they will strive to gain more to become generalizing specialists.

● **Team lead**: The team lead is a host leader and also the agile coach, responsible for facilitating communication, empowering them to choose their way of working, and ensuring the team have the resources they need and are free of obstacles.

● **Architecture owner**: Owns the architecture decisions for the team and facilitates the creation and evolution of the overall solution design.

Further roles could be added to supplement these core roles to address scaling issues, including: subject-matter experts (both technical and business as required), enterprise architecture, release management, and third-party security testing.

Earlier versions of DA included a separate *elaboration* stage, between *inception* and *construction*. This is now incorporated into construction.

Summary

- Most agile project frameworks are compatible with most agile delivery frameworks.

- Scrum is a delivery framework based on repeating iterations (called sprints).

- Scrum is where the roles of product owner and scrum master originated.

- In Scrum, the iteration is called a sprint, with a sprint planning meeting, sprint review and sprint retrospective at appropriate times in the sprint – the daily stand-up is the daily scrum.

- In Scrum, the iteration plan is called the sprint backlog.

- Kanban is a delivery framework based on creating and improving a flow of items.

- In Kanban there is less focus on adopting a new framework and roles wholesale, and more of a focus on seeking to improve and evolve from your current ways of working.

- In Kanban there is no formal iteration – there is a more regular replenishment meeting in place of iteration planning, a service delivery review to review performance with stakeholders, and the daily stand-up is the daily Kanban meeting.

- Scrumban is a hybrid approach combining the structure from Scrum with the pull-based flow from Kanban.

- Extreme Programming (XP) is a rich source of technical practices that have become mainstream in most organizations, irrespective of their delivery framework – such as pairing, swarming, Test-Driven Development, refactoring, and the original user-story format.

- Feature-Driven Development is a less well-known delivery approach based on cutting iteration length to the size of the feature – while this allows for more complete work to be deployed, it is harder to plan around as it varies so much.

- Disciplined Agile is a "build your own framework" approach based on using all other frameworks as a common library of techniques to pick from based on need.

14 Trends in project management

New for this third edition, this chapter explores what else is happening in and around the project management world that has an impact on our roles.

Trends in project management

Publishing the Agile Manifesto in 2001 (see page 14) was a *call to action* for the project management profession to progress beyond the *waterfall era* (see page 22). That growth and evolution have continued, and Chapter 11 details new approaches to product development that see many organizations moving beyond projects.

This chapter explores the background to some of the future trends in project management thinking, and how these are likely to impact those working in agile organizations or at least in agile teams.

Developing organizational resilience

The level of turbulence our organizations are experiencing is at an all-time high. There is an ever-increasing pace of change in technology, consumer expectations, regulation, and workforce. Add to this the impact of natural disasters, global financial crises, and pandemics. The contributory factors to this turbulence are often referred to by the acronym VUCA:

- **Volatile:**   This pace of change leads to...

- **Uncertain:**   our context being less predictable, meaning...

- **Complex:**   it's harder to get to the root cause, which in turn...

- **Ambiguous:** increases the risk of misreading the situation.

Organizational resilience is the ability to recover quickly after being disrupted, and learning how to survive and even thrive in challenging times. To develop this resilience, our organizations need to learn how to respond more adaptively by increasing the focus on customer satisfaction and employee wellbeing. This needs an easily understood vision, greater transparency around decision-making, and reducing complexity as far as possible.

Developing project resilience

Projects are also subject to disruption, both internal and external. To cope with this we need to develop our proactivity, flexibility, and persistence, which will help mitigate the impact of disruption.

With proactivity we can anticipate and influence what happens. Having flexibility means we can mitigate disruption by allowing change while still ensuring our projects meet the objectives. Finally, with persistence we can better cope with stress and have the grit to keep going in the face of adversity.

Developing resilience in the profession

The project management discipline is evolving to provide the tools and thinking patterns to be ready for this. For example, since the second edition of this book was published, the Project Management Institute acquired Disciplined Agile (see page 192-193). This is equipping the profession to better deal with these increased levels of turbulence.

The trends outlined below and detailed in the following pages will also help improve our ability to lead successful projects.

Remote and hybrid project teams

Organizations are embracing the hybrid workplace, with a mix of people working remotely and in the workplace. We need to adapt how we set up and support our teams to be healthy and effective.

Emotional intelligence and people skills

Today's workforce has very different needs relating to fulfillment. We need to understand and accommodate these differences to provide an environment where people feel safe and motivated.

Organization change management

Our projects only realize their benefits when new capabilities have been fully operationalized, and this needs people to have the capability and capacity to make these changes. We need to take responsibility for change management from the outset.

The value management office

Organizations are streamlining into value streams and continual flow (see Chapters 9 and 11). We need to adapt to better support how our organizations identify, deliver, and realize value.

The multi-speed delivery model

While organizations are embracing iterative and incremental approaches and shifting to continual flow, many still have a need for plan-driven programs. We need governance frameworks that are able to support multiple delivery speeds.

Storytelling

Effective communication is an essential skill, especially with today's more complex challenges. We need to become better storytellers, communicating our mission as a compelling story, bridging knowledge gaps, and simplifying complex or ambiguous topics.

Working remotely means a location different from the normal workplace – another office, at home, or even on vacation.

Remote project teams

Working remotely is not a new concept. Many knowledge-work companies have supported this for years and it was becoming increasingly popular, even before the worldwide pandemic forced many people to work from home.

As organizations started to bring people back to the workplace, many found that there were benefits to continued support for remote working. This has now become so prevalent that it has evolved into a more **hybrid model**.

The hybrid workplace

In a hybrid workplace, some people work primarily from home and some from the workplace, but mostly people are alternating between remote and the workplace. Improvements to connectivity and tools have enabled entire organizations to shift to these more hybrid ways of working.

This can reduce property costs and also gives employees a better work/life balance. In turn, this helps improve engagement and potentially gives organizations access to a larger pool of talent. While that could sound attractive, some organizations and teams have found supporting hybrid and remote teams a challenge.

The importance of face-to-face contact

With the emphasis on face-to-face collaboration given by the Agile Manifesto, it can feel like a hybrid workplace would get in the way of an agile team working effectively together.

However, those principles were borne out of a time when technology didn't support real-time exchange of significant amounts of video, sound, and data. In 2001, the thought of creating collated teams felt revolutionary to many organizations.

Times have changed. Now, teams can have live video streams, along with persistent chat, screen sharing, and digital whiteboards.

It is even possible to host large group events online – like **quarterly review and planning** sessions – with multiple teams taking part simultaneously. Teams gather into main sessions to hear significant messages, then spread into breakout rooms to discuss and collaborate within their team.

So, while teams may not all be present in-person any more, they can still communicate and collaborate in a very face-to-face way.

Additionally, agile ways of working support hybrid workplaces with the core agile values of empathy, wellbeing, communication, and collaboration. Consider the following to reinforce this:

Assume remote first

Whenever there are several people in a physical meeting room and others connecting remotely, it can be very hard for those not in the room to contribute on an even footing.

Hybrid teams have had great success holding these meetings with everyone connecting digitally, even those in the actual workplace.

Plan slack time and breaks

Although many of us were accustomed to back-to-back meetings, shifting to working remotely meant we were constantly dropping from one call to join another. This leaves no time to decompress. When the whole day is like that, the lack of movement can reduce the flow of blood and oxygen, affecting our ability to think clearly.

Encourage the team to:

- Schedule meetings for 45 minutes, instead of an hour.

- Block out a half-hour every 2-3 hours.

Take these moments to move around, hydrate, and look out of the window. This should make collaborative sessions more effective as well as freeing up more time for creative problem-solving.

Look for opportunities to build empathy

Working remotely also means we cannot stop by a coworker's desk to chat, grab a coffee, or go to lunch. These unplanned meetings help develop our understanding of each other and develop empathy. In a hybrid workplace, look for other opportunities for the team to interact like this, such as online social events.

Keep learning

Hybrid workplaces are new for many organizations. Don't assume we will get it right straight away. We should prepare to make a few mistakes as we learn, be transparent about what works and what doesn't, and be ready to try new ideas as they emerge.

This is an exciting time. It is good that agile values, principles, and ways of working provide such a good foundation for the behaviors we need to make a success of the hybrid workplace.

Emotional intelligence

Emotional intelligence (EQ – see the Don't forget tip) describes the skillset that enables us to recognize and regulate our own emotions and understand the emotions of others. It helps us to build relationships, reduce stress, and defuse conflict, and has the potential to increase team productivity.

Emotions themselves are neither good nor bad, they just are – what matters is how they affect us and how we respond.

It is not uncommon for someone with a high IQ to have poor people skills – offending others easily, struggling to change, and being defensive. In contrast, those with high EQ tend to be more resilient, avoid taking things personally, and collaborate well.

Why this matters to project managers

Successful project managers engage hearts as well as minds. A strong EQ enables us to make better connections with team members and build a safe and healthy project environment.

Fortunately, EQ is a skillset that can be practiced and improved upon, by focusing on the following areas:

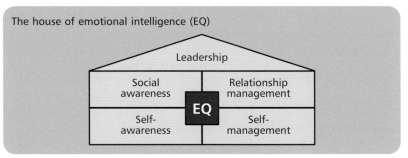

The house of emotional intelligence (EQ)

Self-awareness

We cannot make change without awareness – this is the foundation for EQ. Self-awareness is the ability to understand our own emotions and how they affect our performance. We need to develop our ability to recognize our feelings, especially if we ever find ourselves reacting in unusual ways.

● Watch out for physical changes: tightness in the stomach, tension in the neck, flushed in the face.

● Try to name the feeling – e.g. angry, upset, or scared.

● Reflect on how the feeling impacted our behavior and what could be behind our feelings.

Self-management

Once we are aware, we need to master how we respond so that we can make rational decisions rather than reacting. Self-management is the ability to regulate impulsive feelings and behaviors, manage our emotions in healthy ways, take initiative, follow through on commitments, and adapt to changing circumstances.

Practice mindfulness, being fully in the present, accepting feelings when they occur, and pausing before reacting to get time to think.

Social awareness

Now we "know" ourselves, we are better able to read others. Social awareness is the ability to pick up on the emotions of others; to actively listen. This involves empathy, suspending judgment, and putting ourselves in another person's place.

> "Before you criticize someone, walk a mile in their shoes. That way when you criticize them, you're a mile away and you have their shoes." Jack Handey

Relationship management

Good relationships with our team and stakeholders play a critical role in any project. Relationship management is the ability to manage our interactions well, building on awareness of our own emotions and those of others.

This requires clear communication and effective handling of conflict, building a bond with others over time.

Selfless leadership

Communicating well is critical for understanding the emotional tone of the team. Selfless leadership is the ability to build a safe and healthy environment by motivating, guiding, challenging, engaging, and supporting the team to develop for themselves. Project managers with high EQ:

- Celebrate the team's success, never claiming it as their own.

- Keep the team motivated and focused.

- Are a role model, live the team's values, avoid gossip and stereotyping, deliver what they promise, and help others in building relationships and developing their own EQ.

Change management

All projects involve change, be it a simple process change or a major strategic transformation. The focus of project management is typically on how we deliver this change, so it often neglects the influence people have on achieving the intended outcomes. As discussed in Chapter 5 (*Delivering for impact*), there is a difference between deploying a solution and fully realizing its benefits. The job is not done until the solution has been operationalized.

Change management provides a reliable approach to the people side of change, supporting project delivery by identifying the steps needed to enable employees to move from existing practices to the improved, desirable future state. Change management closes the gap between project delivery and project success.

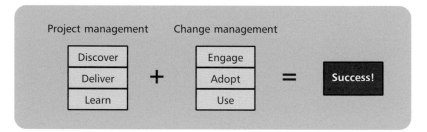

Why this is important
Realizing the business objectives of any project is directly or indirectly linked to employees using new capabilities, following new processes, or adopting new ways of working. In today's value-driven business environment, delivering projects on scope, budget, and on time is no longer enough. Effective adoption of a solution is equally important, if not more so.

After all, what's the point of implementing a new capability if it is not used as intended, or optimizing a new process if it is not followed? Every organization has examples of projects that did not land well, capabilities that were not used, or initiatives that were not sustained.

While change management and project management are separate disciplines, success of the project, return on the investment, and ultimately realizing its benefits are often dependent on the effective integration of both. By making change management a vital part of project management, organizations will adopt new solutions more quickly, enabling them to respond faster to market changes while minimizing impact on productivity.

How this impacts project managers

Change practitioners are far too often only engaged toward the end of a project or when something is going wrong – for example:

- Planning communications, training, and documentation close to when the new capabilities should be operationalized.

- Needing intervention when deployment is delayed because people impacted by the change are not ready for the change or do not have the capacity and capability to adopt it.

Change management is a team effort. It is better to collaborate with change practitioners on a unified approach, engaging them right from the start to think about the timing and change activities across the whole project. This is based on the same reasoning as building in quality from the outset (see pages 80-81).

Many projects will not need the support of a full-time change practitioner and many organizations do not have a dedicated change management team. This means the project manager and others in the team have to be informed and ready to plan for and deliver change enablement activities as well.

Change management in an agile context

Agile project management succeeds by making work items small, delivering frequently, and enabling fast feedback and learning.

Lean Change Management similarly delivers effective outcomes by breaking the main transformation into small increments of minimum viable change, and typically delivering in monthly iterations. This enables change plans to adapt as new requirements are uncovered. It also aims to codesign how the change will be implemented with those affected by it. The framework is best illustrated by its *lean change cycle* (see below).

Planning ahead for change management is not the same as detailed planning up-front – it should still be iterative and incremental.

203

Lean Change is the best change approach for agile projects – visit **leanchange.org** for more information.

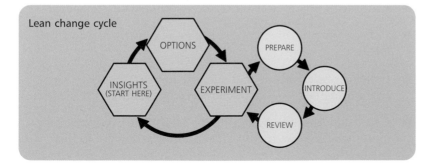

Lean change cycle

The value management office

When organizations have multiple portfolios and programs of work, it's important to provide oversight and guidance to ensure that everything is run well. Typically, organizations establish a project management office (PMO) with a team responsible for setting and maintaining standards for project management.

The traditional PMO typically focuses on how best to manage the triple constraints of scope, cost, and time (see page 12) or extend this to also include quality, risk, and benefits (see page 144). It defines appropriate mechanisms for communications, risk, quality, and stakeholder engagement. However, this over-emphasizes how the work gets done rather than ensuring outcomes are delivered, which might be summarized as:

> "Nice landing, shame it's the wrong airport." Anon

Focus on value over deliverables

We need to better align with and support the move toward value streams (see Chapter 9) and continual flow (see Chapter 11). This means adapting our focus from how well we deliver capabilities to how well we enable and realize benefits from those capabilities once they have been fully operationalized.

This suggests a new relationship with the rest of the organization. We should replace the PMO with a **value management office** that acts as both coach and facilitator to help the organization to:

- Establish their value streams and shift to a continual flow.

- Define an objective model of value, balancing benefits to the end user, the purchasing customer, and the organization.

- Define the benefits, objectives, and key results by quarter.

- Categorize potential work to help optimize use of budgets.

- Objectively prioritize, to identify good returns on investment (ROI).

- Establish mechanisms that support transparency in monitoring and tracking benefits enablement and realization.

- Learn and improve, by facilitating large-scale retrospectives, identifying improvements, and coaching teams to do this themselves.

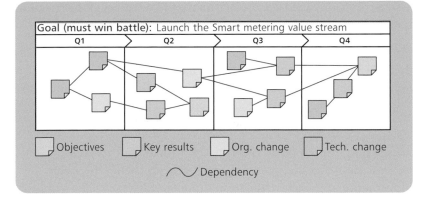

Benefits value mapping

Benefits value mapping helps focus and align programs of work with outcomes and annual goals, and captures dependencies.

1 Identify objectives that will achieve a major goal and map them to an appropriate quarter.

2 For each objective, elicit the benefits expected as key results, mapping these to when they might be realized.

3 For each key result, capture any new capabilities required as organizational and technical changes.

4 Map out the dependencies, noting that a single change could deliver more than one key result.

This becomes a potential queue of work. It should be prioritized as objectively as possible and fed into the appropriate value stream, or approved to receive the funding and a team to initiate a project.

Progressive earned value reporting

The **Earned Value Management (EVM)** approach provides a sound mechanism for illustrating the release of value from projects. However, this is traditionally based on cost or schedule.

By basing this on a more objective model of value, portfolios, value streams, and projects can track their progress on enabling benefits. This should be reinforced by regularly confirming whether benefits are realized.

Benefits value mapping can be done at all levels: the whole organization, a business unit, or even an individual team.

Check out our companion ebook **Earned Value Management in easy steps**.

The release burn-up (see page 37 is also an effective way of tracking delivery of value.

See also the *Pace-Layered Application Strategy* (see page 11).

Multi-speed delivery

This book is intended for project managers wanting to understand how to lead projects with agile frameworks or continual flow.

However, the reality for most organizations is that all projects don't all sit in one bucket. They will have longer-term programs, iterative and incremental work, and potentially continual flow too.

In organizations like this, we need a way to see all our work in a single portfolio. Letting these different types of projects run in isolation of each other is a recipe for increased overheads for synchronizing and orchestrating between them. The Lean Governance approach outlined in Chapter 12 (page 175) will help when working with a multi-speed portfolio.

The highway metaphor
It can help to envisage a multi-speed portfolio as a highway:

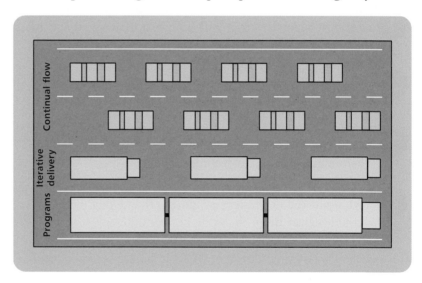

- **Road-trains**: Programs link many deliverables together into a single big batch – while it may take some time to get up to speed, it can be cheaper to deliver some things in bulk.

- **Light vans**: Iterative projects carry smaller batches that can easily be delivered to different destinations – pausing after each delivery to replan the route for the next delivery.

- **Courier cars**: In a continual flow, individual items can be picked up and delivered on demand – going wherever needed at a moment's notice.

Transferrable practices

Whichever speed is determined to be right for the work, it would still be helpful to follow the agile ways of working covered earlier.

This is sometimes referred to as *wagile* or even *water-scrum-fall*.

- **Many iterations, one delivery**: Even when projects are limited to delivering in one big batch, it can still be useful to adopt an iterative development approach – by releasing incomplete increments to a trusted group, you can get early feedback on the work, rather than waiting until the end.

- **Cascaded delivery**: Where analysis or deployment has to be separate, consider breaking it into several overlapping batches – as one batch moves into development, start analysis on the next; as the first batch moves into deployment, move the second into development and start analysis on the third.

- **Quarterly synchronization**: Longer-term programs will benefit from pausing to synchronize with agile projects around the **quarterly review and planning** cycle – there will often be dependencies, and this provides an opportunity to replan.

- **Visualizing the work**: Every project will gain from making all its work transparent – find a way to visualize different types of work, reflecting what stage it's at and whether it's blocked; this will help with communication and problem-solving.

- **Regular stand-ups**: Whether working separately or in cross-functional teams, people will benefit from sharing progress as well as any risks or impediments they can see.

- **Regular retrospectives**: Avoid the trap of waiting until the end of a project to complete a post-implementation review – pause at regular intervals (monthly or shorter) to consider what's working and what could be better, and identify any improvements you can make immediately.

- **Primary stakeholder**: Try to have a distinct role representing the interests of stakeholders and customers – most often, this can be a business analyst.

- **Team coach**: High-performing teams need a safe working environment for morale and focus – as project managers we should develop our coaching and facilitation skills; in the meantime, look to the services of an experienced team coach.

Storytelling

Storytelling is a key skill for project managers. Stories are inspirational and make a message personal and relatable. Careful use of metaphors and understanding the power of what language conveys is key to stories and conveying intent.

Whether you're coaching a team, representing your project to executive stakeholders, or communicating with customers, you will be more effective through the stories you tell.

Storytelling for project managers

There are many circumstances where knowing how to spin a yarn will help:

- **Coaching and mentoring**: Project teams express their culture in the stories they tell. We can use stories to coach, to build morale, and even to troubleshoot.

  For example, when faced with an seemingly insurmountable problem, consider telling a story about how you led another team overcoming a similar challenge on a past project.

- **Pitching a project**: While not promoting the ideas of *governance as a performance art*, it is helpful to be able to tell a compelling story about the impact you hope your project will achieve for the organization.

  A good technique is to keep the story simple, and connect it to what matters to your audience – whether that be sales, profit, market share, or environmental impact.

- **Executive-level presentations**: It is common to experience anxiety when asked to present to senior leaders or the board. Preparing a good story can ease that burden.

  Avoid drowning people in wordy slides. Instead, use powerful images, keep data short and punchy, and leave the narrative to what you say – and practice, practice, practice.

- **Your brand**: They say that your brand is what people say about you when you are not in the room. This can work for you or against you, depending on what people remember.

  In the noisy and turbulent environments we work in, make it easier for people to remember what your project is achieving by providing them with great stories.

Basic story structure

All good stories have a few basics in common:

 Set the scene, introduce the main characters, and explain the circumstances.

 There will be a series of challenges for the main characters to overcome.

 Then, there will be a critical turning point, a key action, or a decision that needs to be made.

 Once made, the action rolls on toward the conclusion.

Of course, the early challenges may be more significant, the main characters may have to go through personal transformation, or the critical decision is put off for too long. Sometimes, the ending is not what was hoped for, but there could be learning. From all of this comes the drama and the intrigue that hooks the audience.

Creating your story

To start drafting your story, consider the following template:

Storytelling canvas

In the past:

> *Recall what life used to be like; honor the past*

and we liked it because:

> *Acknowledge the positive impact (on customers, culture, morale, etc.)*

But then one day/over time:

> *What has changed? Accept that disruption has happened*

and because of that:

> *What impact is this change having? (on customers, culture, morale, etc.)*

So, now we need to:

> *What are you hypothesizing will change and how will you know it has worked?*

leanchange.org/elements/story-telling-canvas

This technique comes from *Lean Change Management*.

Summary

- There is increasing concern about how we cope in a world disrupted by volatility, uncertainty, complexity, and ambiguity.

- Organizations are responding by developing resilience in how they recover quickly after being disrupted.

- We've developed resilience in our projects by adopting more agile ways of working, delivering small increments frequently, getting feedback, and being ready to change when what we're doing is no longer hitting the mark.

- We also need to develop more resilience in our profession too, with a number of options explored.

- We need to adapt to work better with remote and hybrid project teams – this became more common under COVID-19, but now organizations are embracing the hybrid workplace as part of "new normal" ways of working.

- We need to get the most out of our teams and stakeholders, and increasingly this means we need to develop our emotional intelligence (EQ) – especially when some team members seem to have very different needs and motivation relating to fulfillment.

- Although project success is dependent on any new capabilities being fully used as quickly as possible, we need to up our game by working more closely with organization change managers or even upskilling ourselves to take on more responsibility.

- As organizations switch to value streams and continual flow, the role of the traditional project management office needs to shift to becoming a value management office that can support how organizations identify, deliver, and realize value.

- The reality in a lot of organizations is that they will still be running large programs of work alongside agile projects and maybe even alongside continual flow too – our governance frameworks need to stretch up and down to accommodate all the variations into a multi-speed delivery model.

- With communication and engagement being so critical to our success, it can help to learn some storytelling techniques – this will help us communicate our vision better, bridge gaps between people, and simplify complex or ambiguous topics.

Index